The POUM:
Republic, Revolution and
Counterrevolution

Praise for
The POUM:
Republic, Revolution and Counterrevolution

"*The POUM: Republic, Revolution and Counterrevolution* is an analysis of the origins and evolution of a party that represented the best of a generation that played a leading role in the fight against fascism and in "one of the most profound social revolutions of the 20th century". It is history and vindication of a party that fought against fascism to the end and that confronted and fell victim to the caricature of socialism represented by Stalinism".

> **Jaime Pastor** is a retired lecturer in political science, an activist with Anticapitalistas, and a member of the editorial board of *Viento Sur*.

"The history of the POUM is that of thousands of men and women who fought to transform the world; who participated in one of the most profound revolutions of the 20th century. Most of them worked in the factories and fields of Catalonia.

Historian Andy Durgan highlights this often-overlooked fact in the opening lines of the prologue to his latest book. This essay is particularly recommended for anyone who is currently witnessing how the extreme right is destroying consciences in our societies and who is looking to the past for clues to help them understand the present and the future".

> **Marià de Delàs** is journalist and former editor of the daily *Publico*.

The POUM:
Republic, Revolution and Counterrevolution

Andy Durgan

Resistance Books, London
and the International Institute for
Research and Education, Amsterdam

The POUM:
Republic, Revolution and Counterrevolution

El POUM. República, revolución y contrarrevolución, was published by Sylone and Viento Sur in July 2025

Many thanks to Mike Eaude for his extremely useful comments on this text and to David Fagan for translating the Spanish version to English.

Cover design: Adam di Chiara

ISBN: 978-1-872242-48-4 pbk
e-ISBN: 978-1-872242-49-1 e-pub

Published November 2025
by Resistance Books (London)
resistancebooks.org - info@resistancebooks.org
and the International Institute for Education and Research
(Amsterdam) iire.org - iire@iire.org

The POUM: Republic, Revolution and Counterrevolution by Andy Durgan is issue 81 of the *Notebooks for Study and Research* published by the IIRE.

Contents

Prologue

The Workers' Party of Marxist Unification (POUM) was founded on 29 September 1935 from the merger of two dissident communist organizations, the Workers' and Peasants' Bloc (BOC) and the Communist Left of Spain (ICE).

The history of the POUM is the history of thousands of men and women who fought to transform the world, and who participated in one of the most profound revolutions of the 20th century. Most of them worked in the factories and countryside of Catalonia. Like many working-class people of the time, they were educated within workers' and popular cultural organizations. Organization was an integral part of their lives. The membership of the POUM and its forerunners was no exception. Víctor Alba, in his history of the POUM (*El marxismo en España*) explains that:

> The Bloc was an extension of [the member's] home, and for the members working for the Bloc, was more important than the work that provided them with food, as it gave their existence meaning and purpose. The Bloc's local headquarters were packed every day, starting at seven in the evening, when the factories and shops closed. For the members, it was inconceivable to spend an evening doing anything unrelated to the

Bloc. Even Sundays were dedicated to the Bloc. Friends... were all from the Bloc, or you tried to recruit them to the Bloc... There were entire families affiliated to the Bloc.

Furthermore, it was a party with a fairly young membership. On the eve of the Spanish Civil War, many POUM members were under 23—the voting age in Republican Spain. Its two best-known leaders, Joaquín Maurín and Andreu Nin, were 40 and 44 years old respectively in 1936. Members considered them "old."

This short book tells the story of this revolutionary youth, their party, their ideas, and their tragic fate. A story more relevant than ever today in a world also threatened by the darkest reaction, where it's hard not to see parallels with the 1930s.

1

Context

The Workers' Movement

To understand the history of the POUM, it is first necessary to briefly consider the context in which it operated: the workers' movement of its time, the years of the Republic and the Civil War, and the trajectory of international communism.

In the early decades of the 20th century, the Spanish state was economically and socially backward compared to its neighbours. It was also a country with a workers' movement that had a long and militant history.

Within this workers' movement, the communists, including those of the POUM and its predecessors, were overshadowed by their anarchist and Socialist rivals. Spanish and Catalan anarchism, deeply rooted in industrial Catalonia and rural Andalusia, had its origins in the 19th century. It was never a homogeneous movement. In the early 1930s, three basic currents within anarchism can be identified: anarcho-syndicalism, which considered unions the foundation of a post-capitalist society; an anarchist purism that advocated a society based on free communes; and what was called "anarcho-Bolshevism," a relatively small grouping, which advocated armed direct action as a method to end social injustice. Neither tendency was exclusive of the other. All were present in the mass trade union organization, the National Confederation of Workers' (CNT), which had been founded in 1910. Some of the more radical anarchist affinity groups would form the Iberian Anarchist Federation (FAI) in 1927 with the aim of strengthening anarchist influence in the CNT. It would be wrong, however, to classify the vast majority of union members as "anarchist." Rather, the anarchists' methods of struggle and organization fitted the needs of certain sectors of the working class, victims of employer intransigence.

One thing all the anarchist "families" had in common was their apoliticism. Their rejection of politics resonated with a working class whose political rights were denied and who were victims of state repression. The corrupt and unrepresentative nature of the political system before 1931 also posed an obstacle to the anarchists' rivals, the Socialists, who aspired to gain a foothold in the institutions of an undemocratic regime.

The Spanish Socialist Party (PSOE) was founded in 1879. Like other sectors of the European Socialist movement at the time, it embraced a very mechanical version of Marxism, according to which sociopolitical transformation was inevitable. The PSOE remained little more than a sect until the gradual entry in the early years of the twentieth century of a few Socialist representatives into parliament and local municipal councils.

The Socialist trade union federation, the General Union of Workers (UGT), was founded in 1888 and pursued a more moderate and legalistic orientation compared with its anarchist rivals. Until the 1930s, it struggled to expand its influence beyond the mining and centres of heavy industry in the north of Spain. Its participation in the institutions of Primo de Rivera's dictatorship (1923-1930) contributed to deepening the rift between the UGT and its anarchist rivals.

The Republic

The Republic was established on 14 April 1931. Until mid-1933, it was governed by a coalition of the PSOE and petit bourgeois Republican parties. Its reformist intentions, however, were systematically obstructed in Parliament by the minority of rightist MPs.

Outside Parliament, union membership grew dramatically. Confident in their strength and optimistic about the new political situation, the unions, especially the CNT, called a series of strikes to improve working conditions long ignored by employers and the State. In response to these protests, the Republican government resorted to repression, but rather than blunt working-class militancy it only inflamed the situation further. In this context of spiralling protest and repression, the more radical anarchist sectors, many of them members of the FAI, eventually took control of much of the CNT. Such was the social polarization that the CNT defence committees, in the hands of the anarcho-Bolsheviks, were able to initiate armed uprisings in January and December 1933, resulting in dozens of deaths, hundreds of arrests, and the closing down of many unions.

Meanwhile, disillusionment with the 'bourgeois republic' would increase in the Socialist ranks, transformed by the large influx of new members, especially among landless day labourers' in the south. At the same time, the threat of fascism, increasingly present both internationally and in the Iberian Peninsula, further radicalized the Socialist movement. In mid-1933, a "revolutionary" Socialist left emerged, led by veteran UGT leader Francisco Largo Caballero, with a strong base in the unions and the Socialist Youth Federation (FJS).

The electoral victory of the Right in November 1933, partly thanks to the anarchist abstention campaign and the disunity of the Left, made the establishment of an authoritarian regime a real possibility. The right-wing Republican government of the Radical Party depended for its survival on José Mª Gil Robles's Spanish Confederation of Autonomous Rightist Groups (CEDA). A conservative and authoritarian mass Catholic party, the CEDA saw the Nazis' rise to power in Germany through "legal means" as a model for destroying the democratic republic.

Faced with the threat from the Right, different workers' organizations, but without the support of the anarchists and the Communist Party, formed the Workers' Alliances. In Asturias, the Alliance included the CNT, and it was here, when the CEDA joined the government on 4 October 1934, that the revolution would erupt. The Asturian commune, and its bloody defeat after three weeks of struggle by the miners, would be both an example of the workers' movement's resilience and a warning to the ruling classes that it would not be so easy to dismantle the Republic from within.

The commune was defeated by the failure of the movement in the rest of the state. Only in Catalonia did an uprising begin. The blocking by the Spanish constitutional court of the Catalan government's (the Generalitat) cultivation contracts law, which would have improved the situation of the vast majority of the most important section of the Catalan peasantry, the *rabassaires* (vine growers), meant the revolt in Catalonia overlapped with the struggle for national rights. On 6 October, the Catalan President Lluis Companys, leader of the Republican Left of Catalonia (ERC), declared the founding of the "Catalan State within the Spanish Federal Republic." It lasted ten hours before succumbing to the Spanish army.

At the end of 1935, the Republican government, riddled with corruption, called new elections for 16 February. With the electoral victory of the Left, organized in the Popular Front, the workers' movement set out to recover the conditions lost since 1933. In the rural areas of the south, without waiting for the long-awaited agrarian reform, massive occupations of large estates began. The Right reacted to its defeat by completely abandoning any attempt to protect its interests through democratic means and opted to organize a military coup to finally put an end to the Republic and smash, once and for all, the workers' movement. The Republican government, in the hands of petit bourgeois parties, feared the mass movement as much as, if not more than, the Army officers plotting to overthrow it and took few measures to prevent the uprising of 18 July.

Civil War

The swift victory the military rebels had hoped for failed to materialize, thanks to the reaction of the workers' movement, which took to the streets to oppose the uprising. Antifascist militias, formed within a few days by workers' organizations, managed to bring more than half the country under their control, including almost all the major urban centres. In many places in what would become the Republican zone, the military uprising sparked a social revolution, with its epicentre in Catalonia. Many workers and peasants were not fighting to defend the bourgeois Republic, but to create a new world. The masses proceeded to take over the organization of daily life. One of the most visible symbols of this great transformation was the unprecedented entry of women into political and social life.

Real power was in the hands of a myriad of committees and armed groups. The revolution went furthest in Catalonia with the widespread collectivization of industry and services. Agrarian collectivization, which had its most radical expression in eastern Aragón, soon occupied by the CNT militias, also spread to Andalusia, Castile and the Valencia region. In Asturias, the workers' organizations exercised control over both the economy and the war effort.

In contrast to the CNT and POUM, the Popular Front parties, Republicans, Socialists, and Communists, opposed the revolution. Instead, they presented the war as a defence of democracy against fascism. This, they argued, was the only way to win the support of democracies and the middle classes. In the case of the Republicans, and at least in the more social-democratic sector of the PSOE, opposition to revolution, whatever the circumstances, concorded with their politics. Another matter, as we shall see, was the Communists' defence of the bourgeois Republic. The first step towards this reconstruction of the state was the appointment of a new government headed by Largo Caballero on 4 September 1936. One of the most urgent tasks was to organize the war effort. The militias were thus converted into units of the new Popular Army with its hierarchies and traditional military discipline.

The military strategy adopted by the Popular Front government was determined by its policy of presenting itself to the world as a "normal" bourgeois democracy. The essentially orthodox strategy pursued by the Republican Army was doomed to failure, given that it faced an enemy heavily armed by the fascist powers. During the course of the war, the rebels' allies, Fascist Italy and Nazi Germans, sent weapons, aircraft of all types, and thousands of technicians and advisors. Italy also sent around 80,000 troops. In Spanish-occupied Morocco, up to 80,000 mercenaries were recruited to serve as shock troops for the rebels.

The Republic, in contrast, suffered the effects of "non-intervention" promoted by Great Britain and France, which meant that not only could the Republican government not obtain weapons from the democracies or, in theory, anybody else. The Republic's ports were consequently blockaded by the navies of the signatories of the pact to prevent the arrival of arms. The pact was also signed by the very same fascist powers that were sending vast amounts of military hardware to the rebels. The argument that the Popular Front policy was necessary in order to win the support of the democracies is, thus, not supported by the facts. The democracies were never going to support the Republic, whatever its political orientation.

An alternative, and revolutionary, military strategy would have included the massive mobilization of the population (as would happen during the Battle of Madrid in November 1936), a defensive, positional war, using lightning raids and more limited incursions, combined with guerrilla warfare, thus avoiding massive clashes between two armies with markedly unequal capabilities. At the same time, measures such as the declaration of Moroccan independence, military support for the Moroccan nationalist movement, and the declaration of land distribution to peasants could have contributed to undermining the enemy's rear guard. However, without a workers' government, such a strategy would never be attempted.

Both the CNT and the POUM opposed transforming the war into a struggle solely for the defence of democracy. They believed that the war and the revolution were inseparable (and they did not prioritize the revolution over the war, as many books on the Civil War claim). The problem was that the anarchists had no strategy to ensure that this would be the case. The workers' control of much of industry, land and urban space, and the anarchists rejection of "politics", led them to believe the revolution existed as a "fact in itself". But the working class did not control the army, finance, trade, or communications. They did not control the state.

The anarchists, given their opposition to all states, which they considered repressive bodies, opposed on principle the creation of another state to replace the Republican one. However, the CNT recognized the need to coordinate the fight against the fascist enemy and, lacking any other alternative, ended up collaborating with the Popular Front. Thus, with the military situation increasingly critical, four anarchists joined the Republican government in early November 1936. During the following six months, the anarchist ministers undoubtedly rendered a great service by, effectively, covering up what was really happening: the reconstruction of the bourgeois Republican state.

To end the revolution, it was necessary to undermine its power in Catalonia. The street fighting of early May 1937 would represent a mortal blow to the revolutionary process. The formation of a government headed by the moderate Socialist Juan Negrín a week later, without the participation of the anarchists, represented the definitive reinforcement of the bourgeois state. The last bastion of the revolution would be the Council of Aragón, in anarchist hands, which would be dissolved in August. In February 1938, the CNT, now fully committed to collaborating with the Republican State, returned to the government. The war now dominated everything. The Republican troops' heroism could not overcome the great inequality in material available to both sides. Final defeat, increasingly inevitable, as it would be terrible, arrived in April 1939.

From Lenin to Stalin

The defeat of the Spanish Revolution, and specifically the tragic fate of the POUM, cannot be understood without understanding the context of the degeneration of Soviet communism and, by extension, the communist parties under its sway.

The seizure of power by the Soviets (workers, peasants, and soldiers councils) in October 1917, led by Lenin's Bolshevik Party, inspired a great upsurge of revolutionary movements internationally. In this context, in 1919, the Communist International, better known as the Comintern or Third International, was founded as the leadership of the world revolution. The communist parties, in the process of formation in many countries, would be the national sections of a great world revolutionary party. In the Spanish state, the Communist Party of Spain (PCE) was founded in November 1921, from two splits within the PSOE, against the backdrop of great social unrest (the "Bolshevik biennium" in the rural south, 1918-1921, and the workers' struggles in Barcelona, 1919-1921).

The Bolsheviks, immersed in a disastrous civil war and with a shattered economy in a vast, poor, and essentially agricultural country, were very clear that socialism could only triumph in the new Union of Soviet Socialist Republics (USSR) with the expansion of the revolution to the industrial West. The failure of the world revolution would leave the new Soviet state isolated. With its social base—the working class—decimated by the civil war, the collapse of industry, and the incorporation of many working-class cadres into the state administration, the new regime became, in effect, a dictatorship of the Communist Party.

After Lenin's death in January 1924, faced with the limited possibilities for the revival of the international revolutionary movement, the Soviet leadership, increasingly dominated by the new General Secretary of the Soviet Communist Party (CPSU), Josef Stalin, opted to build "socialism in one country." The principal opposition to this policy, and at the same time in defence of restoring democracy both in the Soviets and within the party, would be led by Leon Trotsky, organizer of the October 1917 insurrection and founder of the Red Army. Trotsky, and the Left Opposition he led, would end up being suppressed. Expelled from the party in 1927, two years later Trotsky was expelled from the USSR. He would fight in exile, until his assassination in 1940, to rebuild communist internationalism. According to the Stalinist dictatorship, "Trotskyism" would become the root of all evil. Any opposition or setback in the construction of "socialism" would be the responsibility of Trotskyism.

Internationally, despite the emergence of groups opposed to Stalinism, of which the POUM was one of the most significant, the bulk of the Communist base remained loyal. The image of the USSR as the world's first Socialist country, and of Stalin as Lenin's heir, was powerful, especially in the context of the failure of social democracy and the rise of fascism.

Meanwhile, the Comintern had become the transmission belt for the Soviet government's foreign policy, and the local communist parties had become its executors. In 1935, the Comintern adopted the policy of the "popular front against fascism," a front that would include both workers' and middle-class liberal, and even conservative, parties. This new strategy represented a 180-degree turn from the previous policy of the "Third Period" (1928-1934). After the "First Period" (1917-1923) of the "revolutionary offensive" and the "Second Period" (1924-1927) of "capitalist stabilization," a new (third) period supposedly began, characterized by the threat of war against the USSR and of a revolutionary offensive by the working class. Politically this new period was reflected in the sectarian and ultra-leftist orientation of the Comintern and, by extension, its national sections. Communists would now refer to the social democrats as "social-fascists" and consider them the principal enemy of the working class; a political line that would lead the official Communist movement to underestimate the danger of Nazism in Germany, with catastrophic consequences.

The Comintern's shift towards the Popular Front was conditioned, above all, by the need to contain the threat posed by Nazi Germany to the very survival of the USSR. Such a threat made it urgent to create, at an international level, an alliance with the democracies, especially France, against the fascist powers. The Popular Front was the national expression of the needs of Soviet foreign policy. Therefore, the uniform adoption of this new orientation by the Communist parties was not based on any analysis of the sociopolitical situation in each country. However, compared to the previous disastrous policy, it was at least in line with the need to confront the threat of the extreme Right and would result in a surge in Communist influence in many countries.

Stalinist Intervention in Spain

At the beginning of the Civil War, the USSR decided to send only non-military aid to the Republic and was even one of the signatories to the Non-Intervention Pact. This policy was short-lived. The massive supply of war material by the fascist powers to the military rebels seriously threatened the Republic's survival. A fascist victory in the Spanish state would pose a threat to Soviet interests in Europe, as it would strengthen the power of Nazi Germany. Thus, despite belonging to the Non-Intervention Committee, Stalin's government decided to send weapons to Spain and also approved the organization of the International Brigades. During October 1936, the first shipments of aeroplanes, tanks, weapons, and ammunition arrived in the Republican zone, along with the first advisors, pilots, and tank crews. Over the next two years around 2,000 Soviet military personnel would be sent to Spain. Along with them came several dozen agents from the secret police, the NKVD, and the military intelligence services.

The arms shipments would not be free. Not only would 80% of Spain's gold reserves be sent to the Soviet Union to pay for them, but the Republic was also substantially overcharged. Due to the logistical complexities inherent in shipping material thousands of kilometres, this aid could never match the far greater military aid and human resources sent by the fascist governments. But the inconsistency of this aid was not only due to logistical reasons. Stalin, rather than seeking a clear victory for the Republic, sought to prevent its defeat before the onset of the increasingly inevitable general conflict in the rest of Europe. A hasty victory for the Republic, with a government under Communist influence (though not a Communist government as such), could constitute another obstacle to a Franco-Soviet agreement against the German enemy. Neither did the Soviet government want a revolution that could have been seen as an alternative model to the Stalinist dictatorship in the USSR.

The Soviet Union's material support for the Republican resistance would contribute significantly to transforming the PCE into the strongest organization in the Republican zone. Likewise, the party's opposition to the "excesses" of the revolution and the defence of private property would gain it support among the petit bourgeoisie. It's defence of an orthodox military policy won over many loyal army officers to its ranks. By mid-1937, the PCE already had some 300,000 members, ten times more than on the eve of the war; the Unified Communist-Socialist Youth organization (the JSU) 250,000; and the Catalan Communist Party, the Unified Socialist Party of Catalonia (PSUC), over 50,000.

However, the reasons for the Communists' newfound power were not limited to their political moderation. Until mid-1935, the PCE, like the anarchists, left-wing Socialists, and dissident communists, defended revolution as the alternative to the "bourgeois Republic." The persistence of this image and self-identification as being a "revolutionary party", "the party of the Russian Revolution", with its discipline and "Leninist" structure, meant that only the PCE and the PSUC, and not the liberal and reformist sectors, were able both to put an end to the social revolution underway in the Republican zone, and to direct politically the war effort of the Popular Front.

Seen in this light, the Popular Front could be considered a necessary tactical interlude, a preliminary phase to the implementation of socialism. The fact that the PCE, despite its commitment to defending Republican democracy and its opposition to the revolution of 19 July 1936, spoke, both during and after the Civil War, of the need for a "new type of democracy," a "people's revolution," and even a "revolutionary war," reflected the situation in the Republican zone.

A central tenet of the Spanish Communists' politics during the Civil War was its campaign of slander directed against the "Trotskyists" of the POUM. The specific nature of this campaign can only be understood in the context of the dramatic situation in the USSR. The systematic use of vilification and lies was part of the scaffolding of terror of the police state that the USSR had become. In the midst of the Spanish Civil War, the great purges had begun, with the physical elimination of many of the remaining members of the Bolshevik Party from Lenin's era and the massacre of hundreds of thousands more Soviet citizens. Between July 1937 and November 1938, according to Soviet sources, 1,575,259 people were arrested, 81% of them for "political crimes," of whom 681,692 were eventually executed.[1]

1 Schögel, Karl, *Moscow 1937*, Polity, Cambridge, 2012, p. 501.

2

The Two Teachers

Joaquín Maurín

Joaquín Maurín and Andreu Nin were not only the two main theorists of the new party, but they would also stand out as the most capable Marxist thinkers in the Spanish state of their time. Maurín would be the undisputed leader of the BOC and the POUM, as secretary general of both parties and their only parliamentary deputy (from February to July 1936). A prolific propagandist, he wrote a multitude of articles in the press, especially for the organizations to which he belonged, pamphlets, and three of the most important books of the 1930s, written from a Marxist perspective: *Los hombres de la Dictadura* (1930), *La revolución española. De la monarquía absoluta a la revolución Socialista* (1931) and *Hacia la Segunda Revolución. El fracaso de la República y la insurrección de octubre* (1935).

Maurín was born in 1896 in Bonansa, a farming village in the Aragonese Pyrenees. At the age of 15, he went to Huesca to study teaching, where he also began his political commitment to a regionalist, social and decidedly anti-clerical version of Republicanism. In 1914, he moved to Lleida to work at the secular Liceo Escolar Laico. Like many progressive young teachers of the time, Maurín was influenced by Ferrer i Guardia's Modern School and directly participated in the pedagogical renewal movement that was taking root in Catalonia. It was in Lleida that Maurín began to emerge as a political figure in his own right, both for his writings in the Republican press and as a talented speaker, establishing a reputation that would later lead the anarchists to refer to Lleida as "Mauríngrad."

1917 would be a decisive year in Maurín's political development. First, due to the general strike of August of that year, when the workers' organizations collaborated with the Republican movement in an attempt to force the democratization of Spain's corrupt political system, which would bring Maurín into contact with the nascent workers' movement in Lleida; and second, due to the Russian Revolution.

In December 1919, while in Madrid doing his military service, Maurín attended the CNT's historic second congress. Inspired by the upsurge in social struggles and the spectacular growth of its unions, and impressed by the revolutionary achievements in Russia, the congress decided to provisionally affiliate to the new Communist International (the Comintern).

During the congress, Maurín met Andreu Nin, marking the beginning of their friendship and close political collaboration. In the spring of 1920, upon returning to Lleida, Maurín was elected provincial secretary of the CNT and appointed editor of its newspaper, *Lucha Social*.

A group of trade unionists soon formed around Maurín and Nin who saw the CNT as a vehicle for emulating the Bolshevik victory in the Spanish state. During the spring of 1921, this group's influence increased when, with the arrest or murder of several veteran Catalan trade union leaders, Nin was appointed national secretary of the CNT. In April, the National Plenum of the CNT decided to send four delegates, including Maurín and Nin, to the Third Congress of the Comintern and the founding congress of the Red International of Labour Unions (RILU) which were to be held in Moscow three months later. It was there that Maurín and Nin would meet the giants of the revolution, including Lenin himself.

Upon returning to Catalonia, Maurín replaced Nin, who had remained in the USSR, as national secretary of the CNT. The newspaper *Lucha Social* became a fervent defender of the Russian Revolution. The trip to Soviet Russia would be key in Maurín's evolution towards communism, although not towards the PCE, which was still weak at this time, because he continued to believe that the construction of a mass communist party in the Spanish state would come through the CNT.

The CNT's relationship with the international Communist movement, however, would be short-lived. In the months following the founding of the RILU, information about the persecution of the Russian anarchists by the Soviet government increasingly reached the Spanish state and in June 1922 the CNT broke with Moscow. As a result, Maurín's group began to collaborate more closely with the Spanish Communists, which led to the formation of the Revolutionary Syndicalist Committees (CSRs). Affiliated to the RILU, the CSRs defended the unity of all revolutionary tendencies (anarchist, syndicalist, and communist) within the CNT and supported "direct action" and "collective violence," while rejecting reformist gradualism and individual terrorism. Their mouthpiece was *La Batalla*, published in Barcelona by Maurín.

The CSR's activities were soon severely limited by Primo de Rivera's coup d'état in September 1923. In a context of growing isolation, Maurín's group joined the PCE in October 1924, becoming the Federación Comunista Catalano-Balear (Catalan-Balearic Communist Federation or FCC-B). The new federation only had about 100 members, including several future POUM cadres.

That the PCE itself valued Maurín's inclusion became clear when, in November 1924, with the support of the Comintern, he was appointed general secretary of the party. But three months later, almost the entire new leadership, including Maurín, was arrested and imprisoned. The repressive context of the military dictatorship, combined with the FCC-B's diverse political origins, made it extremely difficult for the Catalan group to integrate into the PCE, which was now under the authoritarian leadership of José Bullejos, its new general secretary. In 1927, Maurín was accused of maintaining contacts with the former French Communist leader Boris Souvarine, who had been expelled from the French Communist Party for being an oppositionist. In fact, the closest connection between Maurín and Souvarine was actually of a family nature, since, in November 1927, Maurín had married Souvarine's sister, Jeanne, whom he had met during the Third Congress of the RILU in Moscow in July 1924.

Despite the campaign against him, Maurín was still supported by the Comintern and when he was released from prison in October 1927, he went to Paris where he worked for the publishing house of the International and became a correspondent for the Soviet newspaper *Izvestia*. However, the new ultra-leftist orientation adopted by the Comintern in mid-1928 (the "Third Period") would exacerbate the differences between the FCC-B and the PCE. These differences deepened when, in 1929, Maurín argued that because the bourgeois revolution had never been completed in Spain, any revolutionary movement would inevitably be "democratic in character" and, consequently, the PCE should advocate the establishment of a "democratic federal republic." In contrast, following the Comintern line, the PCE itself maintained that the pending revolution should lead to the establishment of a "democratic dictatorship of workers and peasants."[1] Maurín's position was characterised as "right-wing," and given that the FCC-B's leaders expressed solidarity with him, on 5 June 1930, the PCE Executive Committee decided to expel them from the party, denouncing them as "bourgeois agents" and "counterrevolutionary elements." As a result, almost all the FCC-B membership abandoned the PCE in support of its expelled leaders. From that moment on, as an independent communist, Maurín would begin his most fruitful period as a theorist and political leader.

Andreu Nin

Andreu Nin, like his friend Maurín, would become a distinguished writer and disseminator of Marxism. During the first year of the Civil War, Nin would be the principal leader of the POUM. His writings and speeches from this brief period are essential for understanding the development and prospects of the revolution. His assassination by Stalinist agents would make him the most famous martyr of the counterrevolution

Nin was born in El Vendrell in 1892 and began his political activity when he was young. From the age of 13, he wrote for his town's newspaper and in 1909 participated in the great anti-militarist uprising known as the "Tragic Week" (*Semana Trágica*). In 1911, at the age of 19, he joined the Republican Nationalist Federal Union. Already a student teacher, Nin, like Maurín, demonstrated his talent as a pedagogue, writing and giving lectures on the latest theories in progressive education. In 1913, Nin, increasingly interested in social struggles and now living in Barcelona, abandoned the Republicans and joined the Catalan federation of the PSOE.

Like Maurín, Nin became a revolutionary influenced by events in Russia and the great rise of social struggles in Catalonia. In 1918, he joined the CNT. He helped organize and served as president of the CNT's Liberal Professions Union in Barcelona. As a delegate to the CNT's Second Congress in late 1919, he addressed the audience, announcing his resignation from the PSOE, and declared:

I am a fanatic for action, for revolution; I believe in actions more than in distant ideologies and abstract questions. I am an admirer of the Russian Revolution because it is a reality. I am a supporter of the Third International because it is a reality, because above ideologies, it represents a principle of action, a principle of coexistence of all purely revolutionary forces that aspire to establish communism immediately.[2]

While in Moscow, Nin was unjustly accused of participating in the assassination of Prime Minister Eduardo Dato in Madrid and was unable to return to Spain. He remained in the Russian capital for nine years, where he rubbed shoulders with the elite of the Soviet Revolution. This would mark him for the rest of his life.

In Moscow, Nin served as assistant general secretary of the RILU, joined the Soviet Communist Party, and was elected as a delegate to the Moscow Soviet. He travelled to France, Holland, and Italy as a representative of the RILU and was a frequent contributor to its press. One of Nin's tasks was to correct the orientation of Communist trade unionists in a context of a declining revolutionary movement. The radicalism so characteristic of the post-war years could mean the isolation of Communists. Nin insisted on the need to move away from sectarianism and seek maximum unity with the rank and file of the social democratic unions, and even with Christian unions. The ultra-left turn of the Comintern (and, consequently, the RILU) in 1928 put an end to this unitary orientation. The lessons Nin learned during his years in the RILU would form part of his political background for the rest of his life, and he summarized them in his book *Las organizaciones obreras internacionales*, first published in 1933.

In addition to his trade union interventions, Nin was one of the first figures in the international Communist movement to attempt to analyse what he called the "completely new phenomenon" of fascism. After visiting Italy in January 1924, he regularly wrote about the nature of fascism in the press of the RILU and the Comintern. In 1930, his book, *Las dictaduras de nuestros tiempos* was a landmark among contemporary writings on authoritarianism.

In 1925, Nin aligned himself with Trotsky and the Left Opposition in their fight against the bureaucratic degeneration of the Communist movement. He would play an important role in the opposition internationally, although Nin would never be "Trotsky's secretary," as many sources claim. As a result of his Trotskyism, he was gradually removed from many of his political responsibilities. Nin would be the last oppositionist to speak publicly in the USSR when he addressed the RILU congress in March 1928.

Expelled from the CPSU and the RILU, Nin lived precariously and under constant surveillance in Moscow. He helped his imprisoned opposition comrades however he could, and only his status as a foreigner saved him from a similar fate. In the summer of 1930, Nin managed to leave the USSR with his Russian partner, Olga Tareeva Pavlova, and their two daughters. Tareeva had been a dancer with the Bolshoi Theatre ballet and was working in the offices of the RILU when Nin met her. They had married in 1922.

Once back in Barcelona, his life continued to be hard. Only his skills as an expert translator allowed him to survive. Thanks to Nin, classic works of Russian literature, by Dovstoevsky, Tolstoy, Pilnyak, Chekhov, and others, were published in Catalan for the first time. He also returned to political activity in Barcelona, as the principal leader of nascent Spanish Trotskyism.

1   The "democratic dictatorship of workers and peasants" was proposed as the next stage of the Russian Revolution by Lenin before 1917.
2   Cited in Pagès, Pelai, *Andreu Nin Una vida al servicio de la clase obrera,* Laertes, Barcelona, 2011, p. 90.

3

"The True Communist Party"

Division

When the POUM was founded in September 1935, almost 90% of its membership came from the BOC, which had been established in March 1931 with the fusion of the FCC-B and the recently formed independent "Catalan Communist Party". The latter had been organized in 1928 by young activists, some of them from left-wing nationalist background, impressed by the "resolution of the national question" in the USSR, but opposed to the centralism of the PCE. The unified organization retained the name FCC-B until 1932, when, with the incorporation of PCE dissidents in Asturias, Madrid, and Valencia, the Iberian Communist Federation was founded. The BOC had been formed as a broader organization than the purely "communist" Federation, but in practice, the two organizations soon became one.

The BOC was the main workers' party in Catalonia in the years leading up to the Civil War. Its membership grew from around 700 at its founding to around 4,500 when it merged with the ICE four years later. However, its influence stretched well beyond its relatively small membership. It was, for instance, the driving force behind a series of united fronts involving non-anarchist unions, most notably among office and shop workers, printers, metal workers and power station workers. Its role in the formation and leadership of the Catalan Workers' Alliance was another example of the BOC's influence. Maurín was probably right when he estimated that the Bloc had around 50,000 sympathisers by 1934.[1]

The Spanish section of the International Left Opposition had been founded in Liège, Belgium, in February 1930, by a group of exiles led by the Basque Francisco García Lavid (Henri Lacroix). In the following months, the members of this group returned to Spain to take advantage of the new political situation which arose following the fall of Primo de Rivera. At first, the Opposition had few supporters in the Spanish state; however, a number of highly experienced communist cadres joined its ranks, including Nin and Juan Andrade. Both Lacroix and Andrade had been founders of the PCE. In 1932, the Spanish Trotskyist group adopted the name Communist Left of Spain (ICE.) Although it would never have more than a few hundred members, the ICE distinguished itself for its intellectual capacity; its magazine *Comunismo* was the most outstanding Marxist publication in Spain in the pre-war years.

The main differences between the BOC and the Trotskyists lay in their relationship with the international Communist movement and in aspects of their political strategy within the Spanish state. While the Trotskyists considered the degeneration of Spanish communism to have its origins in the development of the international movement, the BOC, at least initially, considered it to be a consequence of poor leadership at a local level. The Trotskyists criticized the BOC's "confused politics: its unclear organizational basis, its call for the CNT to "take power" in September 1931, and its advocacy of "separatism" and the creation of "national movements" in areas of the state where there was little national consciousness (see chapter 4). The BOC press, on the other hand, denounced the Trotskyist opposition as a divisive and irrelevant sect that was "condemned to live on the margins of the workers' movement," a marginality from which it would simply "blindly follow" the positions Trotsky put forward.[2]

From 1933 onwards, the differences between the two organizations gradually diminished, allowing for a gradual rapprochement that culminated in their merger. On the one hand, in late 1932, the BOC clarified its position in relation to the international Communist movement and adopted an openly anti-Stalinist stance. Maurín recognized that the Soviet regime had degenerated as a result of the triumph of the theory of "socialism in one country." A theory that had led to the Comintern's subordination to the Soviet state. The main premises underpinning the BOC's communism now coincided with those already established by the first four congresses of the Comintern, during Lenin's and Trotsky's period of influence.

The BOC now openly defended Trotsky against Stalinist slander, describing him as "Lenin's best comrade," "the man of the October Revolution," possessing "extraordinary courage as a fighter for the communist cause."[3]

Recognizing the degeneration of the Comintern, the BOC advocated not its reconstruction in the short term, but rather cooperation with the "strong minorities" existing in many countries, who wanted to return to the "tradition of Marx and Lenin." By the 1930s, a variety of organizations had emerged, most from within the Socialist and Communist parties, their adherents having been radicalized by the economic crisis, the rise of fascism, the failure of social democracy in power, and the degeneration of the Russian Revolution

In 1933, some of these groups, including the BOC, formed the International Bureau for Revolutionary Socialist Unity (IBRSU, also known as the London Bureau.) For the adherents of the Bureau, the Second International (the Socialists) was "completely burned out," while the Third (the Comintern) had "strangled internal democracy" and with the slogan of "socialism in one country" had "liquidated the interests of the world revolution." But before the creation of a new International could be considered, it was necessary to rebuild the revolutionary parties in all countries. Thus, the Bureau proposed "developing joint international actions between its own sections and other revolutionary sections of the workers' movement, in order to prepare for the founding of a reconstructed International on a revolutionary socialist basis."[4]

Towards the POUM

By 1933, the ICE had entered a crisis, both due to its growing conflict with the international Trotskyist movement and its lack of growth. At most, it had about 800 members, mainly in the Llerena region (Extremadura), Madrid, Seville, and centres in the north of the Spanish state. In Catalonia, it had barely a few dozen members.

Until 1933, the international Trotskyist opposition presented itself as a faction of the "official" Communist movement. It abandoned this pretence only after the German Communist Party, following the sectarian line of the Comintern, had completely underestimated the threat posed by the Nazis, claiming instead that the main danger facing the working class came from the Social Democrats.

From then on, the Trotskyists declared themselves in favour of building a new "Fourth" International. The fact that, a year earlier, the Spanish group had stopped presenting itself as an "opposition" and instead became an independent organization was one of a series of disagreements with the leadership of the Trotskyist movement. As a result, the international leadership backed Lacroix in his attempt to oust Nin as General Secretary of the ICE. Lacroix's expulsion for misappropriation of funds and his subsequent attempt to return to the PCE, whilst denouncing "the masked counterrevolution of Trotskyism,"[5] did not help improve relations between the ICE and the international organization.

These relations deteriorated further in 1934, when Trotsky advocated that his followers join the Socialist parties in order to influence the new leftist movements emerging within them. The ICE rejected the new approach due to its experiences within the UGT, where it had been regularly sanctioned by the union bureaucracy. The Spanish Trotskyists, on the other hand, insisted that the "guarantee for the future" lay in the united front and in "the organic independence of the vanguard of the proletariat"; they had learned these principles from Trotsky and were unwilling to renounce them, "even at the risk of having to walk our path to victory separately."[6]

The events of October 1934 would create a climate within the workers' movement that was very conducive to unity. For the BOC and the ICE, the lack of a mass revolutionary party was the main cause of the workers' defeat. Meanwhile, within the Regional Committee of the Workers' Alliance in Catalonia, Maurín and Nin had already resumed the close collaboration they had enjoyed years earlier.

In its publications, the BOC defended the need to unify all Marxists into a single party, including the PCE. However, this position was essentially propagandistic, hoping to attract at least some of the members of these parties, especially the PSOE (see chapter 5).

Where such an initiative seemed feasible was in Catalonia, where the divisions among the Marxist parties were greatest. In addition, as Maurín pointed out, both the UGT and the CNT, and more recently the Workers' Alliance, had been founded in Catalonia, and given the strategic weight of the region, these organizations had subsequently had a prominent role in the history of the Iberian workers' movement. Thus, at the initiative of the BOC, between February and April 1935, there were three meetings between its representatives and those of the Catalan Federation of the PSOE, the Communist Party of Catalonia (PCE), the social democratic Socialist Union of Catalonia, the radical nationalist Catalan Proletarian Party, and the ICE.

It became clear that reaching an agreement would be very difficult. The two Socialist organizations favoured an initial separate union as a first step towards a general unification. For their part, the Communists declared that political unity should be based on the Comintern's programme. In the end, the BOC and the ICE remained on one side, and the other parties, that would eventually form the PSUC in July 1936, remained on the other.

With the failure of the Catalan unification process, the BOC continued to propose the creation of a unified party at a state-wide level. The ICE leadership, on the other hand, believed that the creation of such a party would only be feasible in Catalonia, given the strength of the BOC, but that in the rest of the country its members should join the PSOE. However, the majority of ICE members rejected the leadership's proposal and instead opted to form branches of the new party throughout the state.

Unification

The BOC and the ICE reached the final agreement to unify both parties in early July 1935. For the ICE, the unification of the two parties had been achieved on the basis of a programme that incorporated "all the fundamental principles" of Trotskyism:

> [with regard to] the international character of the proletarian revolution, condemnation of the theory of socialism in one country... the defence of the USSR, but with the absolute right to criticize all the errors of the Soviet leadership, affirmation of the failure of the Second and Third Internationals, and of the need to re-establish the unity of the international workers' movement on a new basis.[7]

However, reality was closer to Nin's publicly expressed opinion, that unification had been achieved easily because there had been no "fundamental disagreements" separating the two parties, and that "neither side had made any significant concessions."[8]

The BOC's idea had always been to build a revolutionary party "from Catalonia outwards," but in practice, this project had not made much progress. Unification with the ICE gave the Bloc the opportunity, through the new party, to expand throughout the Spanish state. Maurín, in particular, was also interested in the strengthening the party leadership, which depended too much on him, by incorporating Nin. At the same time, the unified organisation would benefit from the presence of the ICE membership, among whom there were many experienced militants, whose contribution would immediately be evident in the party's press.

Due to the two parties having to operate clandestinely after the events of October 1934, a meeting of leaders of both organizations rather than a congress founded the new party. This was held in Barcelona on 29 September 1935, at the home of two ICE members, Francesc de Cabo and Carlota Durany. The new party was to be structured on the basis of democratic centralism, which allowed for the broadest internal democracy but not the existence of permanent organized factions. Supreme authority was to be vested in the party's annual congress, at which the 41 members of the Central Committee and the general secretary were to be elected. Given the impossibility of holding a congress in the short term, the meeting of leaders named a Central Committee composed of 29 members of the BOC and 12 members of the ICE and an eight-person Executive Committee. Maurín was named general secretary. He would continue as editor of *La Batalla*. Nin assumed the position of editor of *La Nueva Era*, the party's theoretical magazine.

In July 1936, on the eve of the Civil War, the POUM had around 6,000 members. Geographical distribution remained uneven. The new party was present in more than 400 municipalities, almost 75% of them in Catalonia, where the Executive Committee stated that in the preceding months, "the pace of party activity [had been] truly extraordinary."[9] The party's strength in Catalonia lay in certain rural areas, especially in the provinces of Girona and Lleida. There were also strong branches in the cities of Girona, Lleida, Manresa, Reus, Sabadell, Tarragona, and

Terrassa, and in large towns such as Figueres, Olot, Sitges, and Vilanova i la Geltrú.

Outside of Catalonia, the areas where the POUM was established were those where the BOC had had a presence: the provinces of Castelló and Valencia, and in the Catalan-speaking areas of eastern Aragon. In the rest of the country, the new party inherited the ICE's groups and the BOC's organisation in Asturias. Before the Civil War, the POUM already claimed to have branches in almost all the Spanish state. The party's growth was reported in its press as being particularly marked in Valencia, Madrid, and Galicia, as well as in Catalonia. As the "sole defender of the Socialist revolution within our proletariat," the POUM was optimistic about its capacity for further expansion. The party was, according to its press, "the great concern of the bourgeoisie," as the Bolsheviks had been in 1917.[10]

The new party presented itself as "the true Communist Party of Catalonia and Spain."[11] For Maurín, Lenin's Bolshevik Party was the model, but:

> A party cannot be a copy, an imitation, an adaptation. It must have a life of its own... (and) to have that life, its roots must go deep into the soil of the country in which it exists. [The task of such a party would be] to fuse the interests of a class with the general interest of a people, with the interests of an entire nation or several nations linked by a single state: that is the secret of every revolutionary movement of historic magnitude.[12]

1   Durgan, Andy, *Comunismo, revolución y movimiento obrero en Catalunya. Los orígenes del POUM*, Laertes, Barcelona, 2016, p. 167.
2   Cited in ibid. p.90.
3   Cited in ibid., p. 88.
4   *Revolutionary Socialist Bulletin*, January 1936.
5   Lacroix to the Central Committee of the PCE, 14.7.33. (PCE Archive).
6   *Comunismo*, September 1934.
7   Letter to the National Committee of the International Secretariat, *Boletín interior de la Izquierda Comunista de España*, 1.8.35.
8   *La Batalla*, 19.7.35.
9   *La Batalla*, 26.6.36.
10 *La Batalla* 17.4.36.
11 Comitè Executiu del POUM, *A propòsit d'un manifest faccional*, 10.12.35, Barcelona.
12 Maurín, Joaquín, *Hacia la segunda revolución*, El Perro Malo, Toledo, 2023, pp. 148, 286.

4

"Marxism as Interpreted by our Proletariat"

The Socialist-Democratic Revolution

Maurín, Nin, and other members of the new party put forward a Marxist analysis of the main socioeconomic and political problems they faced. They understood that the Marxist method was not based on mimicking historical experiences, especially the Russian Revolution, but rather on learning from them. As Maurín explained in late 1934:

> The doctrine of the future great revolutionary Socialist (communist) party ... must be [not] Marxism and Leninism as interpreted by the epigones, but Marxism and Leninism [as] interpreted by our revolutionary proletariat [since] mechanical transpositions of experiences that have occurred in certain countries to others always have disastrous results.[1]

The POUM's vision of the pending revolution in the Spanish state was based on that developed by Maurín since the late 1920s. Marxists of the time, analysing the

Spanish socioeconomic and political situation, questioned whether or not the bourgeois revolution had already been completed. Almost all of them, mostly members of the PSOE, were convinced that it was up to the bourgeoisie, or rather, petit bourgeois Republicanism, to complete this revolution before the proletariat could begin the "socialist stage." Maurín, on the other hand, showed that the foundations of capitalism had already been established in Spain during the 19th century. The political phase of the bourgeois revolution, the "democratic revolution," remained to be completed. It was necessary not only to end the monarchy, but also to implement a profound programme of agrarian reform, "solve" the national question, grant full civil and political rights to women, break the power of the Church, and dismantle the army.

Maurín argued that neither the bourgeoisie as a whole, nor any sector of it, was capable of carrying out this "democratic revolution." He based his analysis on the backward nature of Spanish capitalism, which determined the composition of the ruling classes as an alliance between semi-feudal and bourgeois forces, an alliance that had impeded the development of a true bourgeois democracy.

With the collapse of the monarchy in April 1931, the Republican parties formed a coalition government with the Socialists. But the petit bourgeoisie was also unable to complete the democratic revolution because it lacked the social weight to confront the ruling classes. In addition, the Republicans had not only proved incapable of completing the democratic revolution, but also increasingly repressed popular mobilizations.

For the dissident communists, only the working class, supported, as in Russia in 1917, by the peasantry and national liberation movements, would be capable of completing the democratic revolution and paving the way to socialism. But there were two main obstacles preventing the working class from fulfilling its historic role. First, the absence of a genuine mass communist party to counter the influence of reformist socialism and anarchism and to act as a revolutionary vanguard in the struggle for power. Secondly, the illusions held by many workers and peasants in bourgeois democracy, especially in the period immediately following the fall of the monarchy. To demonstrate to the working class that it had no alternative but to break with the Republicans, the BOC put forward a series of democratic demands that it believed a petit bourgeois government could not, or would not, implement. These demands, clearly of a transitional nature in the context of Spain in 1931, included land for those who worked it, the right to self-determination for national minorities, the nationalization of the banks, and the separation of Church and State.

The events of October 1934 marked a turning point in the polarization between the masses and the ruling classes, which were committed not only to preventing the democratic revolution at all costs, but also to returning to the socioeconomic and political situation that existed before 1931. In this new context, it was more evident than ever that "the democratic Republic, in which the greatest hopes of the working masses, the middle classes, and the petit bourgeoisie were placed, has been completely eroded in a short time, in less than four years."[2] The "definitive fall" of the petit bourgeois parties had already taken place in the general elections of November 1933 when, without the support of the Socialists, its electoral base collapsed.

Since 1931, Maurín had maintained that, by solving the tasks of the democratic revolution, the working class would pave the way to socialism. After October 1934, this transition became clearer: the next, second, revolution would be "socialist democratic" (as opposed to "bourgeois democratic").

The conception defended by Maurín and the POUM in 1935 and 1936 of a "socialist-democratic revolution" was misunderstood, by Trotsky among others, as a revolution by "stages" or as a defence of "democratic socialism" of a social-democratic nature. In reality, there was no difference between the POUM's position and that of the Bolsheviks in October 1917, when the Soviets took power without the completion of the bourgeois revolution. With power in the hands of the working class, they would move directly to the implementation of socialism. As Maurín had concluded at the end of 1934:

> From now on, the struggle is not between Republic and Monarchy, between democracy and dictatorship, between the petit bourgeoisie and the grand bourgeoisie, but more specifically between revolution and counterrevolution. The choice is now: socialism or fascism.[3]

In May, 1936, he clarified that:

> While reformist socialism, Menshevism, claims that the Russian Revolution is a bourgeois-democratic revolution, revolutionary Marxism, represented by Lenin and Trotsky, believes that the proletariat must conquer political power in order to carry out the bourgeois revolution, which the bourgeoisie is incapable of carrying out, and to initiate the socialist revolution...

The seizure of power by the working class in Spain equally:

will entail the realization of the democratic revolution that the bourgeoisie cannot carry out… and at the same time it will initiate the socialist revolution by nationalizing the land, transport, mines, large-scale industry and banking… [thus carrying out] not a bourgeois-democratic revolution, but a socialist-democratic one, or more precisely, a socialist one.[4]

The Agrarian Question

According to Maurín, "the alphabet of the Spanish revolution begins, naturally, with the letter A, and the letter A is the agrarian revolution." The need for sweeping agrarian reform constituted the greatest challenge to the democratic revolution, and the very existence of the Republic depended on its solution. But, as the POUM programme explained:

> It is evident that this great agrarian transformation cannot be carried out by the bourgeoisie, as has been clearly demonstrated in our own country. The industrial bourgeoisie is bound by a dense network of interests to the remnants of feudalism, which constitute the social layer of the large landowners. The Agrarian Reform enacted by the Constituent Assembly [in 1932] was, ultimately, nothing more than a clever ploy to halt the revolution that was brewing in the countryside. The problem is not one of reform, but of revolution.[5]

For the dissident communists, the peasantry as such, unlike the landless rural proletariat, constituted, fundamentally, a petit bourgeois group. But it was impossible for the proletariat, in a country whose economy was dominated by agriculture, to seize power without the support of the peasant masses. The peasantry, in turn, could not carry out the agrarian revolution without the collective power of the industrial working class.

Developing a Marxist agrarian policy in the Spanish state was not easy given the division of the peasantry into day labourers, sharecroppers, tenant farmers, smallholders, and other socioeconomic strata. Among other things, the BOC called for the creation of a public "Agrarian Bank," whose mission would be to provide low-interest loans, the establishment of agricultural schools in all regions, agricultural machinery centres available to farmers, and the cultivation of abandoned lands by state-controlled experimental farms. But the basis of the POUM's agrarian programme, as with that of the Bolsheviks, was the demand for "the land for those who work it," with the expropriation of large estates without compensation. Handing over the land to the peasantry would increase the rural masses' purchasing power, which, in turn, would provide the necessary impetus to shake Spanish industry out of its slumber. At the same time, the POUM hoped that the contradiction between the peasantry's thirst for land and government ineptitude would convince the peasants of the need for a revolutionary solution.

The BOC was able to gain a base among certain sectors of the Catalan peasantry due to both its agrarian policy and to the fact that its members were often at the forefront of organizing the region's rural masses into unions. Even in the wine-growing regions, a stronghold of the ERC-led Rabassaires' Union, the Bloc would have some influence, in particular in the Tarragona region. But, the BOC had its most important base among the peasants of Girona and Lleida, areas where there was a greater variety of types of agricultural property and leases than in the wine-producing regions. Like the *rabassaires*, the peasantry of Girona and Lleida sought, with the arrival of the Republic, to improve their conditions.

The most important peasant base for the dissident communists would be in the province of Lleida, where, at the beginning of the 1930s, 65% of the working population worked on the land. Maurín's group's presence in the area since the days of the newspaper *Lucha Social* in the early 1920s would help the BOC gain influence in the Lleida countryside. From 1931 onward, unrest in the area was on the rise, especially in the central regions of the Pla d'Urgell. At the centre of this struggle was the Provincial Agrarian Union, led by BOC members. On the eve of the Civil War, the union claimed to have some 8,000 members and branches in more than 100 towns, some of which were veritable POUM strongholds.

The POUM's agricultural programme also outlined the policy of the workers' state once the working class had taken power, it:

> ...will give the land to the peasants in usufruct. That is, they will possess it, not own it, since the land will be nationalized, with a single owner: the workers' state. The peasant(s) will have all the land they need to survive... but they will not be able to sell or rent it. The workers' state will organize directly or assist in the... creation of large collective farms, resulting in the progressive industrialization of agriculture, experiments that

will be the beginning of the second revolutionary phase in the countryside, that of socialization.[6]

The National Question

As Maurín commented at the end of 1934:

> Spain today is a collection of peoples imprisoned by a police state. A forced cohesion that is a permanent source of rivalry and antagonism. Spain is united by force, not by its own will... The dissolution of centralism would have greatly helped to eliminate the remnants of feudalism and usher in a new phase in the history of our country.[7]

Maurín insisted on the centrality of the national question in any revolutionary process in the peninsula. His uncompromising defence of the right to self-determination for national minorities clashed with the attitude of much of the Spanish workers' movement of the time, which was generally hostile to national demands.

From a young age, Nin also stood out for his defence of national rights and soon came into conflict with the leadership of the Catalan Federation of the PSOE. His book *Los movimientos de liberación nacional*, published in 1935, can be considered a classic exposition of the question from a Marxist perspective.

Nin had assimilated a Marxist analysis of the question during his stay in the USSR. From such a perspective, he drew parallels between the Spanish state and the Russian and Austro-Hungarian empires, governed by absolutist and despotic governments based on the domination of semi-feudal elements, large landowners, and the Church. In Spain, this coalition of reactionary interests had launched a crusade against Catalan nationalism, thus turning the national question into one of the key factors in the pending "democratic revolution." But since the Catalan bourgeoisie soon abandoned its attempts to gain greater regional autonomy, the fight for self-determination had passed into the hands of the petit bourgeoisie. However, according to Nin, and as would be demonstrated in October 1934, if not before, the petit bourgeoisie was incapable of defeating the Spanish state. Only the working class could complete this task. As "the enemy of all oppression," the working class "would fail in its most basic duty if it did not rise up against one of the most acute forms of oppression: national oppression."

In 1931, in the context of a strong growth of the nationalist movement in Catalonia, Maurín defended "separatism" as a revolutionary element that would accelerate the disintegration of the state, not only in Catalonia but throughout the peninsula. According to Maurín, "the prospects for the socialist revolution in Spain are greatly favoured by the presence of a national problem." Such a movement, Maurín believed, would not appear "to the popular masses of the Peninsula as a separatist movement, but as a liberating uprising with which all workers and peasants would immediately sympathise."[8]

At the beginning of the Republic the BOC's defence of "separatism" would be a strong point of disagreement with the Trotskyists who defended "self-determination," and that only in the Catalan case. From 1932 onwards, given the certainty that it was unlikely, at least in the short term, that movements of this kind would develop outside of Catalonia, the Basque Country and Galicia, the BOC opted for a more orthodox position, demanding "self-determination" of oppressed nationalities rather than their "separation." In turn, the ICE had changed its previous position regarding the fight for national rights in the Basque Country, which it considered "reactionary," and had come to defend, as did the BOC, the need for the Basque proletariat to defend the right to self-determination.

During 1934, with the declaration by the Spanish constitutional court of the Generalitat's cultivation contracts law as unconstitutional, the need to establish a Catalan republic increasingly began to be posed on the Catalan left. Initially, this was another area of disagreement between the two dissident communist organizations. The BOC advocated the creation of a "triple front" of workers, peasants, and the national liberation movement that, fighting for the Catalan Republic, would transform Catalonia into a revolutionary bulwark that would "defeat the counterrevolution throughout Spain, a call to arms, (leading to) workers and peasants across the peninsula joining (a) general insurrection that the counterrevolution would not be able to resist for more than a few hours or days."[9] The ICE, in contrast, took a more defensive stance, demanding support for a Catalan republic only if it were declared. Trotsky, however, argued that revolutionaries should fight to lead any movement to separate Catalonia from the Spanish state.[10]

On the eve of the October 1934 revolt and Companys's abortive declaration of a Catalan republic, Nin adopted a position similar to that of the BOC and Trotsky, urging Catalan workers to "support the national liberation movement in Catalonia" and to strongly oppose "all attempts by reaction to attack it." Later, he considered the proclamation of the Catalan Republic to be an act of immense revolutionary significance. According to Nin, the workers' movement should try to remove the "indecisive and traitorous petit bourgeoisie" from the leadership of the Catalan movement for national rights and embrace the demand for a republic, proposing to "liberate Catalonia from the Spanish yoke, the first step towards the Union of Iberian Socialist Republics."[11]

The convergence between the two organizations over the national question would be reflected in the programme of the new unified party. Strongly influenced by Lenin and the model of the USSR as a supposed "union of free peoples," the POUM insisted that:

> The proletariat can only have one attitude: to support actively the indisputable right of (oppressed) peoples to freely determine their own destiny and to constitute themselves as an independent state if this is their will... The proletariat, a resolute champion of democratic demands, must displace the bourgeoisie and petit bourgeois parties from the leadership of the national (liberation) movements they betray, and carry the struggle for the emancipation of (the oppressed) nationalities to its ultimate conclusion... The struggle for the right of peoples to independence does not represent the disintegration of the workers of the various (oppressed) nations that make up the State, but, on the contrary, their closest union, which is the only guarantee of victory. The recognition of the indisputable right of peoples to determine their own destinies, on the one hand, and the common struggle of the workers of all nations of the State, on the other, constitute the indispensable premise of the future Confederation of free peoples,

which in our country will have to take the form
of the Iberian Union of Socialist Republics.[12]

Fascism

The ruling classes were horrified by the arrival of Republican
democracy, because it meant the intervention of the masses
in the country's political life, and increasingly favoured an
authoritarian alternative. By late 1931, articles by the
dissident communists referring to the threat of a military
coup were already appearing in their press. The August 1932
failed coup attempt, led by General Sanjurjo, the head of the
Carabineros, would confirm the stark reality of this threat.
With the failure of this first attempt to destroy the Republic,
the ruling classes increasingly resorted to the CEDA's
"legalist" strategy to introduce an authoritarian regime.

Faced with this threat, the dissident communists were
almost the only ones who seriously addressed the significance
of the rise of fascism internationally and the possibilities of a
similar movement being triumphant in the Spanish state.
While the anarchists perceived all governments as "fascist,"
without exception, whether Mussolini's Italy, the USSR, or
the Spanish Republic, the Socialists, at least until the end of
1933, underestimated the seriousness of the threat.

Nin, drawing on Trotsky's writings, argued in the
spring of 1933 that although fascism might not be an
imminent danger in Spain, it would be "a crime" for the
workers' movement not to prepare for what could soon be a
real threat. As in Germany, liberal and right-wing
governments had prepared the ground for the far Right with
their repressive policies and the continued presence of
"leading reactionaries" in the state machinery.

At the same time, Maurín drew parallels between the conditions that had produced German fascism and the situation in Spain. The worsening economic crisis in the Spanish state opened the possibility of the development of counterrevolutionary movements akin to fascism. The division within the workers' movement between reformist socialism and "anarchist adventurism" hindered a united reaction of the workers' movement to this threat. The failure of the PSOE to introduce sweeping reform had demoralised the Spanish proletariat. The anarchists, in turn, had taken advantage of this situation to proclaim that the failure was of "socialism" itself. Additionally, in order to develop, fascism also required a "totally reactionary bourgeoisie" and the absence, or elimination, of bourgeois liberalism. Finally, the human material needed for the fascist "hordes" could potentially be recruited from the unemployed or from the various right-wing paramilitary or youth organizations.

However, according to Maurín, there were at least three important factors that clearly differentiated Spain from Germany. First, the workers' movement had not been defeated as it had been in Germany, so the possibility of organizing resistance against the Right remained. Secondly, the petit bourgeoisie, despite the growing problems it faced, had not yet turned its back on bourgeois democracy. Thirdly, a mass fascist party had not yet developed, and the far Right was divided. Thus, Maurín affirmed that any counterrevolution in Spain, as it had frequently had in the last one hundred years, would take the form of a military uprising, but, given the international situation, with "Mussolini-ite and Hitlerite influences." The failure of the Republic to carry out a thorough reform of the army meant the monarchical and reactionary foundations of an oversized officer corps remained intact.[13]

1   Bloc Obrer i Camperol, *Les lliçons de la insurrecció d'octubre*, Barcelona, 1935.
2   Maurín, *Hacia la segunda revolución*... p. 54.
3   Ibid., p. 240.
4   Maurín, Joaquín, "¿Revolución democráticoburguesa o revolución democráticosocialista?", *La Nueva Era, May* 1936.
5   POUM, *Què és i què vol el Partit Obrer d'Unificació Marxista*, Barcelona, 1936.
6   Ibid.
7   Maurín, *Hacia*... p. 84.
8   *La Batalla* 3.9.31.
9   *La Batalla* 21.6.34.
10   Trotsky's comments on the possiblity of a Catalan republic were published for the first time in Spanish in *Inprecor*, November 1984, pp. 50–51.
11   *Leviatán* September 1934
12   *La Batalla* 19.07.35.
13   *La Batalla*, 23.3.33.

5

Socialism or Fascism

Antifascist Unity

Faced with the growing threat of the authoritarian right and the disastrous sectarianism of official communism, the BOC and the ICE advocated the creation of an anti-fascist united front. The united front tactic originated in the Comintern's policy at the end of 1921 as a defensive shift in response to the decline of the post-war revolutionary movement. It proposed building a front with other workers' organizations with specific goals, in which each organization would maintain its political independence.

In Catalonia, the BOC had sufficient influence to promote a series of united trade union fronts in 1933, which popularized the tactic among the non-anarchist sectors of the workers' movement. Among them was the Office and Shopworkers' United Front, which organized an unprecedented strike in November 1933 involving some 80,000 workers. In December, following the right-wing electoral victory, the BOC persuaded the other Catalan workers' organizations, with the notable exception of the CNT and the Communist Party, to form the Workers' Alliance. The Alliance aimed to achieve the unity in action of the working-class movement to confront any right-wing attempt to impose an authoritarian regime by exploiting its parliamentary strength. The Alliance also rejected the "insurrectionism" of the anarchists because it could serve as an alibi to justify "a reactionary and fascist coup to restore order." It also recognized the need to attract the petit bourgeoisie to the side of the proletariat to prevent it from "shifting towards fascism."

In the following months, dozens of similar Alliances were formed at a local level in Catalonia and throughout the State, especially in Valencia and Asturias—the only place where the CNT would participate. The Asturian Alliance declared that the goal of a united working class should be not only to defend itself from the authoritarian right, but also to carry out a social revolution.

In October 1934, especially in Asturias and Catalonia, the Alliances would play a key role in the general strike. In Asturias, they became revolutionary committees and were at the heart of the commune's social and military organization. In Catalonia, led by the BOC, the Alliances forced Companys to declare the establishment of a Catalan Republic. Alliances took control of many towns and announced the creation of the Catalan Republic and, in some places, the Socialist Republic.

In August 1935, the Comintern's shift towards the creation of Popular Fronts represented a break with the idea of a workers' united front. For the POUM, the Popular Front strategy would lead to the proletariat subordinating itself politically to the petit bourgeoisie. As fascism was a consequence of the crisis of capitalism it could not be fought by defending bourgeois democracy. The Comintern's new orientation demonstrated its "total incomprehension" of the nature of fascism and would confine workers' struggle within "a bourgeois framework", thus giving the counterrevolution time to prepare. It was a repetition of "what the Mensheviks wanted in Russia in 1917" and of the position of reformist socialism, the disastrous consequences of which had already been seen in Italy, Germany and Austria.

Even so, the POUM did not underestimate the importance of attracting the petit bourgeoisie to the side of the proletariat. The rise of fascism in other parts of Europe demonstrated that its main base lay within that social class. As Nin would state during the Civil War:

> The petit bourgeoisie, potentially, is neither revolutionary nor reactionary. It wants order, whatever that may be, but still order. And this order can only be established by the proletariat or the bourgeoisie.[1]

Thus, the POUM advocated maintaining the political independence of the workers' organizations while defending "a programme of concrete demands" that demonstrated that the solution to the problems of the petit bourgeoisie could only be achieved if the working masses controlled the means of production and exchange.

With the call for new elections in February 1936, the Socialists opted to reconstruct the Republican-Socialist alliance of 1931, but now with the participation of the Communists, thus forming the Popular Front. Faced with this reality, the POUM unsuccessfully proposed forming a "workers' front" with the other workers' parties, which would then reach a tactical agreement with the Republicans. But both the Socialists and the PCE accepted a direct alliance with the left-wing Republicans, based on a bourgeois democratic programme.

Unable to form a workers' front, the POUM, in late 1935, offered to support a left-wing electoral alliance on the condition that it be temporary and aspire to "defeat the counterrevolution in the elections," secure an amnesty for all political prisoners, and restore the Catalan Statute of Autonomy (suspended after October 1934).

The fact that there was massive working-class support for some form of electoral unity, even if only to achieve an amnesty, was also decisive for the POUM when it agreed to participate in the electoral alliance. The CNT, faced with working class support for unity against the Right and the presence of thousands of its members in jail abandoned its electoral abstentionism and, effectively, encouraged its members to vote.

During the election campaign, the POUM insisted that the pact could not be interpreted as anything other than a purely electoral commitment. The alternative to the fascist threat remained revolution. Maurín, addressing a "euphoric" crowd of 5,000 people in Madrid, in a hall adorned with gigantic portraits of Lenin and Trotsky, declared that:

> On the one side is the socialist democratic front, the republican and workers' front, and on the other only thieves and murderers... We are going to the elections thinking not only of our dead and prisoners, but also of the victory of our revolution that will trace a diagonal line through Europe between Madrid and Moscow that will contribute to the sinking of fascism throughout the world[2]

Jordi Arquer, former leader of the BOC, declared in Barcelona before 12,000 people that the POUM did not oppose "bourgeois democracy to fascism, but [...] communism, the dictatorship of the proletariat."[3]

The POUM hailed the Left's triumph in the elections as a great victory for the workers and peasants and a significant defeat for the counterrevolution. It was not a victory for bourgeois democracy, nor did it represent mass support for petit bourgeois Republicanism but was rather a consequence of the revolutionary struggle of October 1934. The POUM warned that, given the depth of the economic and social crisis, a new left-wing Republican government would be even less able than the one of 1931 to confront the ruling class's resistance to any attempted reforms, however innocuous. The masses were faced with two paths: that of Germany and Austria, or that of Asturias.

"Anti-Marxist Nonsense"

In the months leading up to the outbreak of the Civil War, the call to create a "great revolutionary party" remained the central theme of the POUM's politics. To become a state-wide party, the POUM needed to win over at least part of the left wing of the PSOE. In particular, the dissident communists were optimistic that they could attract to their ranks the Socialist Youth (FJS). The fact that the FJS press during 1934 and 1935 had expressed its sympathy for both Trotsky and the BOC reinforced such optimism.

On a more practical level, the FJS's relations with the dissident communists had intensified throughout 1934. When the FJS leaders, Carlos Hernández Zancajo and Santiago Carrillo, visited Barcelona in September 1934, they offered the BOC's youth organization, the Iberian Communist Youth (JCI), the leadership of a unified youth organization in Catalonia. The offer was rejected by the JCI because the founding of a new united youth grouping could be not separated from the creation of a unified party.

After the events of October 1934, the FJS defended the need to "Bolshevise" the Socialist movement, with the aim of centralizing the party structure and removing "reformists" from all leadership positions. It also rejected any new alliance with the Republicans and advocated withdrawal from the Second International. The question of the "international reconstruction" of the workers' movement could only be addressed "on the basis of the tradition of the Russian Revolution."

The differences between the POUM and the FJS became clear in a series of written exchanges between Maurín and Carrillo, published during July and September 1935. Carrillo reiterated his conviction that the future great Spanish Bolshevik party would be built within the PSOE and called on the BOC to join the party in order to strengthen the Left in its fight against the reformists. Maurín, in response, reaffirmed the BOC's belief that the construction of such a party would be impossible while two irreconcilable tendencies coexisted within the PSOE. For Maurín, the problem was not numerical—that had not worried Lenin in 1917—but rather ideological clarity. Unity was essential, but it had to be achieved on a revolutionary basis, not within any of the existing workers' parties.

The POUM's hopes of attracting the Socialist Youth were in vain. The official Communist movement, revitalized after the turn to the Popular Front and, above all, its call for the formation of a United Party of the Proletariat, proved much more attractive to the FJS than the POUM's revolutionary Marxist orthodoxy. The founding, with the Communist Youth, of the Unified Socialist Youth (JSU) in the months leading up to the Civil War would prove decisive in providing Stalinism with a mass base during the Civil War.

In contrast, the leader of the Socialist left, Largo Caballero, seemed more open to Marxist political unity.

And in April 1936, the UGT leader even proposed to Maurín that the POUM and the PSOE merge. The possibility of this happening was slim given the way the POUM posed the question of unification. Maurín rebuked those Socialists who defended the forming a party in which everyone would have a place. Such a perspective "confused what constitutes a revolutionary party with social democratic parties."[4] It was no surprise that the POUM Executive Committee rejected Largo Caballero's proposal.

By the end of May 1936, the POUM had become convinced that the two principal tendencies of the PSOE (the followers of Largo Caballero and Indalecio Prieto respectively) were not very different from each other. Both agreed with the Popular Front strategy, favoured the PSOE's continued membership in the Second International, supported the League of Nations, had voted for the left Republican Manuel Azaña to become President of the Republic, and accepted the government's permanent suspension of the constitutional guarantees which curtailed workers' rights.

The POUM's frustration with the twists and turns of the Socialist left, especially of its leader, was reflected in an article by the former Basque ICE member, José Luis Arenillas, who lamented that such a significant segment of the working class continued to believe in the "anti-Marxist nonsense" that Largo Caballero was in some way a revolutionary.[5]

The Giant with Feet of Clay

For the proletariat to fulfil its role as the driving force of the socialist democratic revolution, it was necessary, according to the POUM, to overcome two major problems: the

53

division of the workers' movement and the lack of a "coherent revolutionary ideology." Beyond its disputes with other Marxist currents, the central task for the POUM, if it aspired to have a decisive influence in the working class, was to pull towards it sections of the CNT. In Catalonia, the CNT was almost hegemonic among the proletariat, but it was an ideologically and organizationally fragmented movement; described aptly by Maurín as "a giant with feet of clay."

According to Maurín, the great waves of migration from rural areas to Barcelona since the beginning of the century had provided the human material for the development of anarchism in the city. These immigrants, lacking political education or experience in the class struggle, nevertheless demonstrated a "great capacity for struggle." Anarchist propaganda made inroads among these, generally, unskilled masses who lacked stable jobs, especially because there was little opposition to libertarian ideas within the emerging labour movement.

For Nin, inspired by Lenin, the dual absence of large workplaces and a socialist political alternative had perpetuated the influence of anarchism. Small workplaces, which were prevalent in Barcelona, weakened collective strength and gave rise to a polarization between passivity and direct action, and even terrorism. Such attitudes would supposedly disappear with the creation of large-scale industry and the emergence of a working class educated in the spirit of cooperation and discipline prevalent in modern factories. Thus, anarchism enjoyed little support in places where heavy industry and large concentrations of workers predominated, such as in Vizcaya, or in countries like Germany, Great Britain, and the United States. Like Maurín, Nin stressed the lack of a revolutionary alternative to anarchism as explaining the latter's influence. As Nin would explain in 1937:

> Anarchism is the punishment suffered by the workers' movement for its opportunist sins. Workers have followed the anarchists because they saw in them the revolutionary spirit of their class, which they did not find in reformist socialism. If, instead of the Socialist Party, a Bolshevik party had existed in Spain, anarchism would not have taken root.[6]

According to the dissident communists, the CNT had been unable to capitalise on the large strike movements at the beginning of the Republic due to its leaders' "lack of revolutionary theory." Because of their apolitical nature, the anarchists did not see the need to "seize power" and, faced with widespread mobilization, had done little more than tail end the spontaneous actions of the workers.

In the BOC's opinion, at a time when it was necessary to strengthen trade union organization, the anarchists were dedicated to destroying it with their insurrectionary policy of "revolutionary gymnastics", while excluding those opposed to this orientation. Between 1931 and 1933, the CNT leadership, dominated by anarchist groups, launched a series of unsustainable strikes and three insurrectional movements. At the same time, its sectarianism led it to persecute any tendency within the unions that disagreed with its strategy, leading to a more moderate faction, the *treintistas,*[7] splitting away and forming its own Opposition Union federation, with over 60,000 members, based mainly in the industrial periphery of Barcelona and in Valencia.

Many BOC trade unionists also left or were directly expelled from the CNT for participating in electoral lists.

The expulsion of these members often led to the withdrawal of their union from the CNT. Other unions, influenced by the BOC, left the CNT in disagreement with the anarchists' radicalism and sectarianism. Along with unions organized directly by Bloc members during the first years of the Republic they founded in May 1936 the Workers' Federation of Trade Union Unity (FOUS) which had around 50,000 members. Its main base was outside Barcelona, reflecting the influence of the POUM, the local federations in the cities of Lleida, Reus, and Terrassa being particularly strong.

After the Popular Front's electoral victory, a major strike movement erupted. For the POUM, this was a sign of the potential for struggle of the working class, especially in Madrid, where the CNT seemed to have begun to displace the UGT in the leadership of the working class—as would become clear during the important construction strike in June. The anarchists' actions contrasted with the repeated calls for calm by the Socialists and Communists, in the face of provocations from employers and the far right. The POUM enthusiastically supported the CNT's activities outside Catalonia, convinced that a widespread mobilization of the masses was the only way to avoid a counterrevolution.

However, according to the POUM, the CNT's role in Catalonia was different. The POUM accused the FAI leadership of the Confederation not only of sabotaging the strike movement in Catalonia but even acting as strike breakers. Anarchists actively opposed the impressive strikes led by the newly founded FOUS in the print industry and among office and shop workers and in the city of Lleida.

The growing prominence of the FOUS would convince the POUM that the new federation would displace the CNT in Catalonia which, according to its own figures, had lost more than half of its membership since 1931. From such a position of strength, the POUM hoped to encourage unity between the FOUS, the CNT, and the UGT. But the POUM had seriously underestimated the social weight of the CNT, as would become clear after the start of the revolution in July 1936.

Towards the Second Revolution

In the months before the Civil War, unrest spread throughout the Spanish state, with a wave of strikes, land occupations in the south, and violent clashes in the streets between gangs of fascist youth and the Left. As the sole POUM representative in parliament, Maurín would be a lone voice warning of the imminence of a fascist uprising and calling for a united, and revolutionary, response from the workers' movement. On 15 April, he asserted in the Cortes that if the Socialists believed, as their German and Austrian counterparts had, that it was possible to "stabilize the democratic republic," they would, like them, witness the establishment of "a fascist regime that will be presided over by Gil Robles, Calvo Sotelo, or another candidate for Führer or Duce."[8]

The Socialist left had vetoed the PSOE's participation in the government, hoping in return that the Republicans would fulfil their assigned role of completing the "bourgeois revolution". According to the POUM, this demand amounted to passively waiting for the petit bourgeois government to "wear itself out completely," and also failed to take into account the illusions that the Popular Front still inspired in broad sectors of the popular masses. The POUM believed that a single-party Socialist government would be appropriate if the PSOE were a "united, revolutionary party and the centre of attraction for the majority of the working masses." Since this was not the case, it was necessary for the masses to experience a "phase of transition" in which a Popular Front government with Socialist participation would be formed. Thus, the POUM challenged the PSOE and the PCE, who "believed in the effectiveness of the Popular Front," to form a government with the Republicans. This would make it clear to the workers that such a government was incapable of confronting the counterrevolution. Once this phase was over, the moment would arrive to establish a true "workers' government."

In the weeks before the Civil War, with the threat of counterrevolution so palpable, the POUM again insisted on the need to rebuild the Workers' Alliances at a local and state-wide levels. The dissident communists also called for the establishment of Alliance committees in the workplaces, elected by all workers.

As the party programme stated:

> The Workers' Alliance in our country, based on the conditions of the workers' movement, will play the role that the Soviets played in the Russian Revolution: organs of first the united front, then the insurrection, and finally as instruments of power. When the working class seizes power, the current bourgeois state must be replaced by something new, the embryo of which is to be found in the Workers' Alliance.[9]

But neither the other Catalan Marxist organizations, which were in the process of unification and in favour of the Popular Front, nor the former *Treintistas*, now reintegrated into the CNT, favoured rebuilding the Alliances.

Meanwhile, the struggle in the streets against the fascist gangs had intensified. Like the other workers' parties, the POUM had its own modest paramilitary structure, the Action Groups. These groups were usually composed of JCI members and acted in defence of party activities, as well as intervening in strikes and against the far right. Many of them would play a leading role in the party militias once the Civil War broke out.

With the threat of a military-fascist coup increasingly evident, the POUM was doing everything possible to convince the rest of the workers' movement of the need for joint action to prevent it. In June, Maurín warned again that "reformism has failed in Spain, just as it failed in Italy, Germany, and Austria. It's not a question of reforms, but of revolution." In his opinion, although:

> the October uprising failed… the lesson was tremendously useful. Our proletariat, in light of (this) experience…, should now prepare itself… to launch, in the short term, a new insurrection that will ensure its victory.[10]

On 12 July, the POUM leadership declared that the insistence on subordinating the demands of the working class to maintaining the Popular Front in a climate of profound sociopolitical instability and mass radicalization amounted to "a crime and a betrayal" whose consequences would be very costly.

On 16 July, Maurín left for Galicia to participate in a regional meeting of the party. He ended up trapped in the fascist zone and would end up imprisoned by the Francoists for the next ten years. He was saved from the firing squad thanks to the tireless work of family and friends on his behalf.

Before leaving for Galicia, he wrote what would be his last article as General Secretary of the POUM and editor of *La Batalla*. He warned once again of the "announcement of an imminent military-fascist coup d'état" and, as he had done on other occasions, predicted (correctly) that Generals Francisco Franco, Manuel Goded, and Emilio Mola would be its leaders.

At the end of 1934, in his book *Hacia la Segunda Revolución*, Maurín had concluded that:

> The regime built around the Monarchy has failed. The bourgeois Republic has failed. Fascism is riddled with contradictions that, for the time being, undermine it. But if the proletariat fails to surpass itself, if it is unable to understand its mission by adopting a correct strategy and tactics, focused on the ultimate goal: the seizure of power, then the current generation will be crushed by the counterrevolution...[11]

Maurín's words would prove terribly prophetic. Eighteen months later, in July 1936, the working masses would be forced to confront their mortal enemy. The revolution had begun.

1   "Proyecto de Tesis Política", Boletín Interior órgano de
    información y discusión del Comité Ejecutivo del POUM,
    Barcelona, 5.4.37.
2   *La Batalla* 14.2.36.
3   *La Batalla* 10.1.36.
4   Maurín, Joaquín, prologue (1.5.36.) to Carlos Marx, *Crítica del
    programa de Gotha* (Barcelona 1936), p.29.
5   *La Batalla* 1.5.36.
6   *La Batalla* 25.4.37.
7   Moderate anarcho-syndicalist faction, referred to as the *treintistas*
    because its manifesto against the strategy of the more radical
    anarchists was signed by thirty (*treinta*) well-known CNT leaders.
    The *treintistas* supported the Workers' Alliances in 1934.
8   Maurín, Joaquín, *Intervenciones parlamentarias*, Barcelona, 1937.
    Calvo Sotelo was the leader of the Bloque Nacional, a far-right
    coalition. His assassination on 13 July 1936, by the Assault Guards
    (republican paramilitary police) was supposedly the trigger for the
    military uprising.
9   POUM, *Què és i què vol el Partit Obrer d'Unificació Marxista*,
    Barcelona, 1936.
10 Maurín, Joaquín, introduction to Lansberg, A., *El arte de la
    insurrección, Barcelona,* 1936.
11 Maurín, *Hacia...* p. 283.

6

Revolution

July 1936

The military uprising was expected at any moment. On 15 July, the POUM Executive Committee decided to mobilize the membership in preparation for the inevitable struggle. Many party members, especially those of the Action Groups, now spent the night in the party headquarters. Others stood guard outside the barracks where they suspected preparations for a coup were taking place.

Meanwhile, the POUM organized, as it had done in October 1934, a Military Committee in Barcelona, led by Josep Rovira, head of the Action Groups and future commander of the party's militias. A medical centre was also set up with party doctors and nurses. The approximately thirty Winchester rifles hidden after the October 1934 uprising were brought out of hiding.

On 18 July, the POUM issued a communiqué, supposedly the only one circulating on the streets of Barcelona that day, warning of the imminence of a coup d'état. That evening, the POUM sent delegations to meet with the other workers' organizations in a failed last-minute attempt to persuade them to form a Revolutionary Workers' Front to lead the fight against fascism. Visits by POUM representatives to the Generalitat and the central police station to obtain weapons were met with evasive or outright negative responses.

Confirmation of the military rebellion in North Africa was expected at any time. Rovira addressed members present in the headquarters of the POUM Military Committee, located in the Teatre Principal in the Rambles, explaining that the situation was different from that of 6 October (1934) given the participation of the CNT. They had few weapons, and the authorities wouldn't give them any because, according to Rovira, they feared the working class more than the military rebels. Although the security forces had not revealed their intentions, if the POUM and the CNT took the initiative, they would "control the situation in a few hours."[1]

Early in the morning of Sunday the 19th, informed that the army had left its barracks, a group of poorly armed POUM members was sent from the Teatre Principal to position itself in front of the nearby Drassanes barracks. The rest walked up Les Rambles towards Plaça de Catalunya. Upon reaching Plaça Universitat, the first clash with the army occurred. Among those killed was Germinal Vidal, general secretary of the JCI. Meanwhile, violent clashes broke out in other parts of the city. POUM members fought alongside the Assault Guards in Plaça de Catalunya and with the CNT in front of Drassanes barracks. Of the 161 dead and 312 wounded identified as part of the anti-fascist forces in Barcelona on 19 and 20 July, eight of the dead and thirty of the wounded were known to have been POUM members.[2]

Due to its relative weakness in the city, the POUM played a minor role in the resistance to the military coup in Barcelona, compared with the CNT. The POUM's participation in the fight against the rebels and their allies was more decisive in the cities of Girona and Lleida, as well as in other Catalan towns. In Girona, an Anti-Fascist Front was formed with the participation of the POUM, the CNT, and the ERC. This mobilized workers and peasants from nearby towns and organized poorly armed groups to patrol the streets and besiege strategic locations held by the army. When news arrived from Barcelona of the insurgents' defeat, the rebellion in Girona began to disintegrate, and many soldiers handed over their weapons to the workers.

In Lleida, as in Girona, on the morning of Sunday 19 July, the army took to the streets, declared a state of war, and occupied key buildings. Among the first to react were groups of young women from the JCI who distributed leaflets announcing the general strike that had been declared by the FOUS, the CNT, and the UGT. Meanwhile, the Assault Guards joined the workers who, despite having few weapons, had surrounded the military rebels in many parts of the city. News of the rebels' defeat in Barcelona would also be, as in Girona, decisive in their surrender in Lleida.

In Valencia, where an atmosphere of unity prevailed after the collaboration of Socialists, *treintistas*, and POUM members in the Workers' Alliance, members from all the workers' organizations fought together against the rebels. Unable to conquer the streets, the insurgents retreated to their barracks from which the anti-fascists did not succeed in dislodging them until early August.

In Madrid, POUM members participated in the assault on the Campamento and Montaña Barracks, and some of them would be among the first to be killed or wounded. From both barracks, they took weapons for the first column of the party's militia.

Where the rebels triumphed, many POUM members, mainly former ICE members, died in the unequal struggle against them, or were executed. Among the victims, were many of the party's claimed 230 members in the Extremaduran town of Llerena, murdered by the Civil Guard. The party's losses would be equally devastating in Galicia, Salamanca, and Seville.

The defeat of the military uprising triggered a sweeping social revolution, particularly in Catalonia, with workers occupying buildings and urban space, and taking control of workplaces and public services. The occupied buildings became union, party, and militia headquarters, cultural centres, and popular restaurants. Vehicles painted with the initials of the anti-fascist organizations careered through the streets in a display of what was termed "revolutionary driving".

The POUM occupied several iconic buildings in central Barcelona, including the Palau de la Virreina, which became the Joaquín Maurín Institute and eventually housed a library of up to 90,000 volumes; the Hotel Falcón (now the Andreu Nin Library) provided accommodation for the party's foreign collaborators; the Hotel Rívoli, served as the headquarters of the Executive Committee; Radio ECP2, which became the POUM's radio station; and the printing press of the Carlist newspaper *El Correo Catalán*, where the party's new daily newspaper, *La Batalla*, would be printed.

The scale of the revolution unleashed by the military rebellion took workers' organizations by surprise. On 24 July, the POUM issued a platform of immediate demands that included a 36-hour work week; a 10% wage increase; a 25% rent reduction; a "progressive revision of the Statute of Catalonia"; the immediate purge of the armed forces; the election of commanders by soldiers and assault guards; the maintenance of armed militias; a summary court martial for the leaders of the fascist insurrection; control of production by factory committees; and the distribution of the lands of large landowners.[3]

The POUM would not clarify its position in relation to the extent of the revolution until 6 August when it published a manifesto describing the multitude of anti-fascist committees, which had emerged in response to the military uprising, as the potential basis of a new revolutionary power.

The Problem of Power

The reaction of the working masses to the fascist uprising had changed everything. As Nin would later point out:

> The roar of cannon fire and the crackle of machine guns that July morning roused from their slumbers workers who still held onto democratic illusions. The electoral victory of 16 February had not resolved the problem facing our country. The fascist reaction resorted to arguments more compelling than the ballot paper.[4]

The POUM had no doubt that the long-awaited socialist democratic revolution was underway. But in a short time, the working class had surpassed the "democratic stage" and moved directly onto the Socialist stage. Nin, now the central leader of the POUM in Maurín's absence, would eloquently summarize the new situation at a large rally in Barcelona on 6 September 1936. Before the war:

> The struggle was not posed... [as] between bourgeois democracy and fascism, but between fascism and socialism, between the working class and the bourgeoisie. And events, comrades, have

proved us completely right. The working class...
blocked the path of fascism in Catalonia on 19
July and has crudely posed the question of
power... the working class of Catalonia and the
working class of Spain are not fighting for a
democratic republic... Five years of the republic
and none of the fundamental problems of the
Spanish revolution had been resolved. The
problem of the Church had not been resolved, the
problem of the land had not been resolved, the
problem of the Army had not been resolved, nor
the problem of purging the judiciary, nor the
problem of Catalonia..., all these concrete
objectives of the democratic revolution have been
achieved not by the liberal bourgeoisie... but by
the working class, which has resolved them in a
few days, with weapons in hand... On 19 July...
not only did feudalism, clericalism and militarism
collapse, but the capitalist economy collapsed
forever.[5]

After the defeat of the military uprising in almost
two-thirds of Spain, power was exercised by countless
committees, many of them based on the parties supporting
the Popular Front, but with the added participation of the
CNT. In Catalonia, the committees reflected the influence
of the revolution. Often called "revolutionary" or "anti-
fascist" committees, their composition depended on the
strength in any given locality of the various organizations.
Generally, the committees were made up of delegates
appointed by the different anti-fascist organizations; few
were elected by the local population. In addition to these
more political committees, there were numerous
committees with responsibility for organizing the militias,

supplies for the front, rearguard security, and, increasingly, industrial and rural collectives.

The Catalan government, unable to manage the situation, proposed to the workers' and Republican forces the creation of a unitary committee to coordinate the fight against the rebel forces. Thus, on 21 July, the Central Committee of Anti-Fascist Militias (CCMA) was formed with five Republican delegates, three from the CNT, three from the UGT, two from the FAI, and one each from the POUM, the PSUC, and the Unió de Rabassaires. Although a majority of its members supported the Popular Front, the CCMA's decisions reflected the weight of the revolution in Catalonia.

In addition to co-ordinating the military struggle, the CCMA took the first steps to control the economy, freezing bank accounts of people who had supported the uprising and implementing measures to help companies already in the hands of workers continue to pay wages. To coordinate security in the rearguard, a Public Order Commissariat was established, with a leading POUM member, Josep Coll, as its general secretary. In August, the Commissariat created the Control Patrols, made up of 700 members of the various anti-fascist organizations. Of these, 325 were from the CNT and 45 from the POUM.

The CCMA's power was concentrated in Barcelona, which gave it considerable influence, but outside the Catalan capital other committees dominated life at a local level. While the CCMA was created on the basis of all anti-fascist organizations, some of the local committees were politically more radical. This was the case in Lleida, where, after dissolving the municipal government, the Committee of Public Safety (a clear reference to the French Revolution) was established, made up, at the insistence of the POUM, only of delegates from the CNT, the UGT, and the principal trade union organization in the city, the FOUS. A local POUM leader, Josep Rodes, took up residence in the civil governor's office as commissar for Public Order. The repression of those sympathizing with the military rebellion in the city would be ruthless.

The influence of the social revolution was also felt in the Valencian region. In Castelló, as in Lleida, a provincial committee was formed without representatives from the Republican parties, with delegates from the CNT, the POUM, and the Socialists. In Valencia, the Popular Executive Committee (CEP), with a clear majority of proletarian representatives, played a role similar to that of the CCMA, and was in charge of military organization, in addition to controlling communications, supplies, public health, and the economy. Nin considered the CEP to be "the government of the proletarian revolution" in the region.[6] However, like the CCMA, the CEP had little success in coordinating the actions of the multiple local committees.

In much of the rest of the Republican zone, regional or provincial committees were created which, like the CCMA, held considerable power during the first weeks of the war. The political orientation of most of these committees reflected the importance of the Popular Front organizations. However, the situation was so polarized that in several places they acted in a markedly radical manner, as was the case with the committees of Cartagena, Gijón, Málaga, and, above all, the Council of Aragón, organized in October and dominated by the anarchists.

The POUM maintained that to consolidate the revolution the working class needed to seize power. But without the CNT, such a goal was impossible. Convincing the CNT of the need to take power, soon became the POUM's main political concern, but it had to overcome the anarchists' conviction that any form of "power" or revolutionary state would inevitably lead to dictatorship. The experience of the Russian Revolution seemed to be the definitive confirmation that this was the case, where Marx's conception of the "dictatorship of the proletariat," as the rule of the majority of the population, had been replaced by the monstrosity of the Stalinist dictatorship.

Nin, in early September, in an attempt to win over the anarchists to the need for a revolutionary power, asked:

> What is the dictatorship of the proletariat? It is authority exercised solely and exclusively by the working class, the abolition of all political rights and all freedom for the representatives of the enemy classes. If this is the dictatorship of the proletariat, comrades, ... the dictatorship of the proletariat exists today in Catalonia....[7]

The dictatorship of the proletariat was not the dictatorship of a single organization but rather "workers' democracy exercised by all workers without exception."

As an alternative to the bourgeois Republic and the Popular Front, the POUM called for the establishment of a Constituent Assembly composed of delegates from workers, peasants, and combatants' committees, not only in Catalonia but throughout Republican Spain. Meanwhile, the POUM argued that the CCMA was potentially the embryo of a revolutionary government in Catalonia. Thus, the POUM proposed to the CNT that the CCMA should become an exclusively proletarian body, without the participation of "the bourgeois parties." This was a proposal the CNT did not accept.

1   Coll, Josep y Pané, Josep, Josep Rovira; *Una vida al servei de Catalunya i del socialisme*, Barcelona, 1978, p. 66.
2   Casas Soriano, Just, Els fets de juliol de 1936 a Barcelona. Els protagonistas i les víctimes, Barcelona, 2016, p. 176.
3   *Avant*, 24.7.36.
4   "Proyecto de Tesis Política", Boletín Interior órgano de información y discusión del Comité Ejecutivo del POUM, Barcelona, 5.4.37.
5   Nin, Andreu, *El proletariado español ante la revolución en marcha,* Editorial Marxista, Barcelona, September, 1936.
6   Ibid. The CEP consisted of 4 Republicans, 2 delegates from the CNT, 2 from the UGT; and one of each from the PCE, POUM, PSOE and the Syndicalist Party.
7   Nin, Andreu, *El proletariado español ante la revolución en marcha*, Editorial Marxista, Barcelona, septiembre, 1936.

7

The POUM and the Catalan Government

The Generalitat Council

Faced with an increasingly difficult military and economic situation, all the anti-fascist forces, albeit from different perspectives, considered it urgent to create a united and solid leadership, both at a military and political level. The Republicans, Socialists, and Communists hoped to reassert the authority of a state seriously undermined by the revolution. The formation of a new government in Madrid on September 4, headed by the veteran Socialist leader, Largo Caballero, was an essential part of this process.

In Catalonia, creating a united leadership would involve ending the existence of two parallel political authorities: the CCMA and the Generalitat. In mid-September, the Catalan government proposed creating a new unified authority, the "Generalitat Council", with the participation of all anti-fascist organizations. The establishment of this new body on 26 September, and the subsequent dissolution of the CCMA, was the logical outcome of the CNT's decision at the end of July not to seize power because it would mean establishing "an anarchist dictatorship." The only alternative the anarchists contemplated was to "collaborate" with the other anti-fascist forces, which would mean subordinating themselves to the Popular Front. The new Catalan government was composed of four Republicans, three anarchists, one each from the PSUC, the UGT, the POUM, and the Unió de Rabassaires, as well as a military advisor.

After acknowledging that no other organization would defend the need to establish a revolutionary government, the POUM justified its participation in the Generalitat Council by arguing that the Catalan petit bourgeois parties had radicalized, the new Catalan government had a "socialist programme," and the workers' organizations constituted a majority within it.

Undoubtedly, the ERC had a mass base, something lacking in much of the Republican movement in the rest of the Spanish state. Many of its leaders saw themselves as social reformers and had established ties with the more moderate sectors of the CNT. Furthermore, a significant portion of the CNT rank and file, despite the apolitical nature of the anarchist activists, voted for the Catalan Republicans in the elections. The continuation of the ERC's "radicalization", according to the POUM, depended on pressure exerted on it by the revolutionary forces, both inside and outside the Catalan government.

The Trotskyists, in contrast, claimed that the ERC was a direct representative of the bourgeoisie. In reality, the left-wing Republicans were, as Trotsky himself would later acknowledge, the "shadow" of the bourgeoisie.[1] The bourgeoisie itself was in the Francoist zone, suppressed or in hiding.

The economic programme, drawn up by Nin, was that of the Catalan Economic Council (CEC), which had been established by the Generalitat on 11 August, and aimed at the "socialist transformation of the Catalan economy." Among other measures, this programme aimed at the "complete collectivization of industry, services, and large agricultural properties," a monopoly on foreign trade, and workers' control of the banks. The POUM compared the new Catalan government to the one headed by Largo Caballero in Madrid, which it defined as a government "against the interests of the revolution." According to the POUM:

> The working-class or non-working-class character of a government will be determined much more by its programme than by its members. ... the Madrid government [for example] has a large working-class majority, yet, judging by its programme and its politics, it is far from being so... A simply anti-fascist government is not enough... As we have repeatedly argued, anti-fascism must be taken to its ultimate consequences, that is to say, to revolution, to socialism.[2]

However, the implementation of the CEC's programme depended on the balance of political forces within the new Catalan government. The number of representatives was similar to that of the CCMA, but the context had changed. Although it was true, as the POUM insisted, that the workers' organizations were in the majority, this included the PSUC, which, along with the ERC, was clearly opposed to the revolution. In reality, the Consell de la Generalitat represented a return to Republican legality, that is, bourgeois legality, despite the "legalization" of many of the revolution's achievements.

The POUM's participation in the Catalan government was also due to its fear of not being see as sufficiently "anti-fascist" by the masses, as well as from being deprived of supplies and weapons for its militias. Even more important was the fact that the POUM believed that joining the Catalan government would prevent the CNT from coming under the influence of the Stalinists and Republicans. For the POUM it was essential to overcome the anarchists' hostility towards the party, which dated back to before the war. The fact that the CNT and FAI in Catalonia had signed a collaboration pact with the UGT and PSUC on 11 August 1936, while refusing to form a liaison committee with the POUM, highlighted the extent of the party's isolation.

The POUM's participation in the Generalitat Council did not mean the party had abandoned its defence of the need for an alternative, revolutionary, power. The new government was purely "transitory" and therefore unlikely to last long. The alternative remained the formation of committees of workers, peasants, and combatants from which proletarian power would emerge.

Andreu Nin: Minister of Justice

The POUM representative in the new Catalan government was Andreu Nin, who was appointed Minister of Justice. During his two months in office, Nin introduced a series of radical measures, including civil marriages that would fall under the responsibility of anti-fascist parties or trade unions; marriage and divorce between two people with equal rights; new legislation to simplify adoption; and the granting of rights of adulthood to 18-year-olds (previously 21).

But where Nin's work would have the greatest impact would be in the area of popular justice. As in all great revolutionary processes, the Spanish Revolution was accompanied by popular terror against those perceived as its enemies. In the first weeks, there was a purge in the rearguard of disloyal army officers, Civil Guards, right-wingers, employers, large landowners, and members of the clergy. To understand this terror, it is necessary to view it in the context of both the long years of repression and injustice suffered by the mass of the population, and the much more ferocious repression in the fascist zone. While in the latter repression was organized systematically from above by the authorities, in the Republican zone it was largely spontaneous. All the anti-fascist organizations, without exception, sought to bring what it described as "uncontrolled" repression under control. The POUM, for instance, had already announced on 31 July that it was the "enemy of individual actions, uncontrolled executions, looting, and pillage. Those who commit these acts dishonour and harm the revolution."[3]

Upon being appointed Minister of Justice, Nin insisted that he would "legislate on what the proletariat is already doing in the streets. Nothing should remain of bourgeois justice." On 13 October, the People's Tribunals were established with the goal of ending arbitrary repression and "guaranteeing the integrity of the proletariat's gains that contributed to its victory in the war." In addition to prosecuting all counterrevolutionary crimes, they were to address acts that "dishonour the revolution," so-called "terrorism" or "house searches that violate orders from the legitimate authorities."[4]

With the regularization of revolutionary justice, there were fewer abuses, and, above all, a decrease in the number of death sentences. Each tribunal was composed of a president and eight members of anti-fascist organizations. Of the seven prosecutors appointed to serve in the new tribunals established in Catalonia, five were POUM members.

The Dissolution of the Committees

Where the new government would succeed in eroding the power of the revolution was in rebuilding the security forces in the rearguard, in imposing greater control over the militias, and, above all, in dissolving the local anti-fascist committees. After the dismantling of the CCMA, the Generalitat Council proceeded to dismantle the local anti-fascist committees and replace them with municipal councils based on the same distribution of representatives as in the new government. In addition, hundreds of other committees, for example, supply, militia, and local defence committees, were also dissolved.

The repercussions of these measures for the revolutionary organizations were obvious. In the local committees of many towns, the CNT and the POUM had been the dominant, and often the only, forces but from then on, power would pass into the hands of the Catalan Republicans and their Stalinist allies. This change was not always accepted peacefully. There were serious doubts, for example, that the Lleida committee would accept its dissolution. A government delegation was thus sent to the city on 30 September to persuade the local committee to comply with the decree. Nin, as Minister of Justice, agreed to accompany the delegation. Members of the local POUM

... received [the delegation] armed, but when they saw Nin, their hearts sank, and they gave in out of party discipline. Nin argued before the Executive Committee [of the POUM] that he had avoided a futile clash, since the POUM alone, and only in [Lleida], could not resist the order to dissolve the committees.[5]

For Trotsky and his followers, the POUM's participation in the Catalan government, meant subordinating the workers' movement to a bourgeois government, and would represent the party's betrayal of the revolution. The dissolution of the committees would be the definitive example of the consequences of this treachery. Nin himself had opposed the dissolution of the committees within the Catalan government. However, once passed, the party's Central Committee saw no alternative to implementing the new decree. This would prove a significant step towards the reestablishment of bourgeois Republican order in Catalonia. As one of the party's leaders, Enric Adroher (*Gironella*), would comment, a few months after the end of the Civil War, the new Government of the Generalitat had had "a single historical mission [...] the liquidation of the committees", while the POUM had been given the task of "convincing the revolutionary forces" outside of Barcelona "of the need to accept that sacrifice, which would turn out to be a further step in the retreat of the revolution". Once this "invaluable service" had been carried out, in December 1936, the POUM was excluded from the Government.[6]

Collectivization

In addition to abolishing the committees, the other key measure introduced by the Generalitat Council to "legalize," if not control, the revolution was the collectivization decree.

The talking over of factories, services and the land by workers and peasants was largely spontaneous. The workers' organizations, in general, followed the initiative of their rank-and-file members. The POUM's initial position was to call for workers' control of production but it soon came to view collectivization favourably, given that it had clearly demonstrated "the socialist spirit of the masses."[7]

Over the following months, the POUM would become critical of the way the collectivization process was being carried out, which increasingly resembled "trade union capitalism" whereby the unions effectively treated each enterprise as their own property. As a result, there were differences in wages and working conditions, and even rivalries and competition, between collectives, even within the same industry. Faced with this situation, the party advocated socialization that would entail the incorporation of collectivized enterprises into a planned socialist economy. It also proposed measures such as the nationalization of banks and a monopoly on foreign trade. The POUM's model was the USSR in Lenin's time.

The debate within the Catalan government over the Collectivization Decree pitted the defenders of the revolution—the CNT and the POUM—against its detractors—the ERC and the PSUC—who attempted to limit recognition only to large collectivizations. In the end, a compromise was reached, according to which collectivized enterprises with more than 100 workers would be recognized, and those with between 50 and 100 employees would be so recognized if three quarters of the workforce voted in favour. In practice, many small businesses, even those with fewer than fifty employees, were collectivized independently of the decree. In principle, the

POUM defended the merger of such small businesses and their socialization but recognized that their "forced" collectivization could turn the petit bourgeoisie against the revolution.

The decree put an end to spontaneous collectivization and paved the way for increased state intervention in the economy. Collectivized companies would now be managed by a board of directors in which the unions, both the CNT and the UGT, were proportionally represented, along with a representative appointed by the Generalitat. Thus, given that the UGT was closely controlled by the PSUC, in many collectives a majority of management was made up of people hostile to the revolutionary process.

Initially, the POUM's attitude towards the collectivization decree was quite positive. According to Nin, the socialist orientation outlined in the CEC's programme was becoming a reality. But the party would become increasingly critical of the decree's limitations. For example, despite being included as a key component in the decree, months later, the credit fund that was so necessary for the functioning of the collectivizations had still not been created. And, above all, the banks had not been nationalized. Differences, for instance, in wage rates and even competition continued to exist between different collectivized enterprises and industries. In short, the decree, according to the POUM, had not overcome the "trade union capitalism" that already existed in many collectivizations.

In March 1937, Josep Oltra i Picó, the party's leading economic expert, would summarize the experience of industrial collectivization in Catalonia as demonstrating:

...that the working class in the workshops and factories is more capable than the bourgeoisie of managing the economy and... improving conditions and increasing the availability of materials... [but] for the working class to be able to develop the new economy effectively, all political power must be concentrated in its hands, without the current interference of petit bourgeois and reformist policies which represent an obstacle to the bold achievements we need in these revolutionary times.[8]

Collectivization also spread to the countryside. As Nin noted in early September:

The land problem has been resolved because workers did not wait for the resolution of this problem through the cultivation contracts law or the Agrarian Reform Institute; instead, the peasants have expelled the landowners and taken over the land.

Rural collectivization had a number of characteristics that were distinct from its urban equivalent. On the Aragon front, the epicentre of the agrarian revolution, the arrival of the anarchist militias was fundamental to the collectivization of the land. The POUM favoured agricultural collectivization but accused the CNT of sometimes carrying it out by force. It was essential to win the peasantry over to the proletariat or at least neutralize their hostility to the revolution. In contrast, forced collectivization was:

clearly counterrevolutionary, as it destroys the indispensable alliance between workers and

81

peasants, undermines the foundations of our economy, plunging the country into hunger and misery, and creates a social climate contrary to the cause we defend.[9]

This was a serious problem in Catalonia, where many peasants favoured land redistribution rather than collectivization. The PSUC took advantage of this situation to champion the Catalan peasantry's property rights.

Upon reaching Eastern Aragon, the POUM militias encouraged peasants to collectivize the land, given the advantages of cooperative work, but it had to be voluntary. In order to orientate its intervention in rural areas, the party organized an agrarian conference in November 1936, attended by delegates from 50 localities. Although the resulting programme advocated the socialization of all agricultural property, it took into account the different forms of landownership among the peasantry. It defended the right to individual cultivation, provided that peasants did not own more land than was necessary for their families. Thus: .

> Small landowners were to continue to cultivate their land, and could work it with their families, but they could no longer own it... The products of their labour could remain in the hands of the producers, but trade could only be carried out through agricultural unions... Collective exploitation had to be encouraged... To this end, model farms had to be created and provided with adequate support.[10]

Wherever it had some presence, the POUM attempted to implement its agrarian policy, but it had lost much influence in the countryside due to compulsory unionization (introduced by the Catalan government in August 1936). The unions under their influence had joined the Rabassaires' Union, which soon came to be dominated by the PSUC. Of the few agrarian collectives managed by the POUM, the most significant was that of the Raimat vineyards in Lleida, which involved 150 families and was presented as a model to follow.

1   Trotsky, Leon, 'The Lessons of Spain: The Last Warning', 17 December 1937, *The Spanish Revolution*, Pathfinder, New York 1973, pp. 309–10.
2   *La Batalla* 17.9.36.
3   *Avant* 31.7.36.
4   *La Batalla* 17.10.36.
5   Alba, Víctor, *El marxismo en España,* Vol. 1, B. Costa-Amic Editor, México 1973, p. 328.
6   Gironella (Enric Adroher), "Sobre los errores cometidos por el POUM", POUM, *L'expérience espagnole*, París, 1939, p. 10.
7   *La Batalla* 27.10.36.
8   Cited in Tosstorff, Reiner, *El POUM en la Revolución española*, Editorial Base, Barcelona, 2009. p. 144.
9   *La Batalla* 19.11.36.
10   *La Batalla* 17.11.36.

8

The People Armed

The POUM Militias

After the defeat of the military uprising in Catalonia, each anti-fascist organization organized its own militia. With this objective in mind, the POUM took control of the enormous Lepanto cavalry barracks in Barcelona, renaming it the "Lenin Barracks." The hastily-formed militias were immediately sent to liberate rebel-occupied Aragon.

The first column of the POUM militia, led by Jordi Arquer and Manuel Grossi, left Barcelona on 24 July. Arquer was a member of the party's Executive Committee and a leader of the Barcelona Office and Shopworkers' Union (Sindicat Mercantil). Grossi, a miner, had been one of the leaders of the revolutionary uprising in Asturias in October 1934. The POUM militia, like most columns at the time, lacked almost all the equipment of a modern army, especially weapons. In addition, most of the militia members had never handled a rifle and needed to be quickly shown how to.

The first permanent base of the POUM militia was in the village of Alcubierre. As in other villages occupied by the militias, one of the first things the POUM column did was organize a committee of local people to govern it. A hospital was also established, as well as the column's headquarters. Relations with the population appear to have been good. Young people from the town enlisted in the militia, and teenagers carried supplies to the positions established by the column in the nearby mountains. Known right-wingers and members of the clergy, who had not managed to flee with the rebels, were arrested, some being executed.

Meanwhile, other groups of militias arrived at the front from different parts of Catalonia. By the end of July, the POUM had already organized seven columns: four on the Huesca front, amounting to around 3,000 combatants at the end of August; one in Teruel, with militia from Castelló and Valencia; another from Tarragona in the Belchite area; and one in Madrid. In August, the POUM also sent 300 militia to participate in the failed invasion of Mallorca.

In Madrid and its surrounding areas, the small POUM militia would participate almost continuously in fierce fighting, in which it suffered a high number of casualties. Its first column would be largely destroyed in early October during fighting in Sigüenza. Meanwhile, in the capital, the Lenin Battalion was organized, with about 250 volunteers. By late November 1936, the small POUM militia in Madrid was led by the Argentine Mika Etchebéhère, probably the only woman to command a militia unit in the Republican zone. Etchebéhère had won the admiration of the militia during the siege of Sigüenza Cathedral in October, from which she who had staged a daring escape. The Lenin Battalion fought on the Madrid front as a separate unit until February 1937 when most of its remaining combatants were killed or wounded during an attack on the fascist position on a hill, the Cerro de Águila, in the Pozuelo sector.

Several hundred POUM militia were also sent to fight on the Madrid front in October 1936 from Valencia and Catalonia. The Catalan column was destroyed near Illescas, in the province of Toledo.

Meanwhile, the POUM militia participated in fierce fighting on the Huesca front during September against the enemy, after some 600 of its combatants occupied the towns of Tierz and Quicena and blocked the Barbastro road. There they withstood the attacks of the much better equipped rebel army, which attempted, from Huesca, to relieve the troops trapped in the rear of the militia on the Estrecho Quinto ridge and in the village of Siétamo.

By early October, Huesca was besieged by the militias, except for a narrow corridor to the west. But the Republican forces in the Huesca area had wasted valuable time trying to occupy secondary positions so when the Republican troops finally launched an offensive against the city on 21 October, they found its defenders well-entrenched. Despite the heroism of the militias, including those of the POUM, the offensive was called off the following day. The failure was due to a lack of coordination between the different columns, a shortage of weapons and air support, as well as the incompetence of the General Staff headed by José Villalba, a professional officer of dubious loyalty. There would be no further attack on the city until June 1937.

Until their dissolution in June 1937, the POUM militias would occupy about 15 kilometres east of Huesca, from Monflorite in the south to Fornillos in the northwest. Initially, their columns were organized into *centurias*, each composed of about 100 fighters, divided into three sections of about 30 militia members, each subdivided into groups of ten, often known as "tribes," whose members generally came from the same town or neighbourhood. Many of the *centurias* were led by members from the party's Action Groups.

Compared to a regular army, an egalitarian spirit permeated the anti-fascist militias, especially those of the CNT and the POUM. There were no symbols of rank. Officers and political commissars mingled with the troops and shared the same living conditions at the front. However, democracy in the POUM militias had some limits. For example, the party leadership was wary of allowing soldiers' committees within their own military units. This apparent anomaly was justified by the POUM leadership by pointing out that the "specific relationship" that existed between party militia officers and the rank and file made any "special rights" unnecessary. It was assumed that the rank-and-file combatants trusted the "revolutionary officers" because they, too, had once been ordinary members of the militia.[1]

POUM militia officers were not elected by the rank and file but rather appointed by the party's military committee. Most POUM militia officers were trusted party members. There were few professional officers. Only the equivalent of sergeants or corporals were elected.

The problem with the revolutionary officers, compared to those of the enemy, was that they lacked "the tactical and strategic skills of modern warfare" and, consequently, "operational and logistical methods" were not applied during the first stage of the war. Only after some of them at spent time in the newly formed People's War Schools (Escuelas Populares de Guerra) would this situation change somewhat. The POUM, which demanded these schools be placed under workers' control, eventually established its own military academy, situated in the collectivized vineyards of Raimat.

Political commissars were also not elected in POUM-controlled units, but rather appointed, like officers, by the party. The Red Army of the early years of the Russian Revolution provided the model for the political commissar for the POUM militias. Their objective was to "maintain the political, moral, and physical health of the troops" in addition to ratifying orders given by officers.

The Military Policy of the POUM

The different militias' initial actions, and not only in Aragon, revealed their limitations. In the case of the POUM militia, despite its effective defence of the Barbastro road in September, it had suffered a crushing defeat with the loss of the village of Leciñena in early October, due to its lack of both experience and arms and to the failure of the neighbouring CNT and PSUC columns to come to their aid.

One of the main problems facing the Republican forces was the need to create a centralized, more effective, command structure. This question was taken up by the POUM almost from the beginning of the war. From their perspective, however, a centralized command structure had to be coordinated by bodies similar to the CCMA, and not the Republican government.

Another problem with such an inexperienced force was the lack of discipline. This problem affected all columns. In an attempt to overcome it, on 2 August, the Military Committee of the POUM militia adopted a disciplinary code that provided for severe penalties for acts of indiscipline. Desertion, for example, would be handled by the Committee and four representatives elected by the militia members, and their decision would be final. Any militia found guilty of looting would be shot.[2]

In September 1936, the POUM introduced its own "militarization" outlined in a "Decalogue of the Militia

Member" in which it declared that "the militiaman must at all times be aware that the cause he defends is that of the proletariat." Therefore, the combatant "will endure with fortitude all adversity arising from the struggle (and) must keep in mind at all times that structuring a new social order is neither a short nor an easy task." Following orders could not imply "in any way recognition of vassalage, but simply a spirit of collaboration to facilitate the task of command." However, in combat situations, they had to obey "blindly" because "to move too hastily to take an objective can cause endless losses in our ranks, and ultimately, the loss of the objective itself." A militia must not forget "that the command has everything planned." Finally, "militiamen must not be cowards".[3]

Of course, declarations and rules alone were not going to bring about a more disciplined attitude. For the first few months, at least, it was political commitment that guaranteed the discipline necessary to prevent the front from collapsing. The high percentage of party members enrolled in the militia—around 80% of volunteers at the beginning—helped reinforce discipline. The presence of the most committed members, especially from the JCI, was more numerous in certain sectors of the front, as well as in sections such as machine gun groups and the artillery. The presence of such activists would be crucial, for example, in the fighting of September 1936.

In October, the militarization of the militias and the creation of the People's Army took place at a state-wide level. Meanwhile, the new Catalan government issued its own militarization decree, which mobilized all men who had completed military service between 1932 and 1935 and subordinated the militias to the Code of Military Justice. In December, the Generalitat established the basis for the formation of the "Popular Army of Catalonia" with its own structures and semi-autonomous status, thus differing from the Popular Army that had operated in the rest of the Republican zone since October 1936.

On the Aragon front, despite the changes introduced by the Catalan government, the situation of the militias would change little. The workers' organizations would maintain their control over the units they led, and the original characteristics of the militias, such as equal pay or the absence of military formalities such as salutes or symbols of rank, would remain unchanged. With militarization, officers were now paid more than the rank and file troops, but in the case of the POUM militia this "extra" payment was handed over to the party.

For the POUM, war and revolution were inseparable. The Communist slogan of "first win the war" was a "simplistic and limited formula" lacking "any solidity or content." What was needed was "war at the front and socialist revolution in the rear":

> ...war is not only won with good weapons, but also with an adequate economy that responds to a revolutionary situation. This economy can only be the result of revolution... The need for general mobilization—especially in Catalonia—is once again on the agenda... The entire civilian population must be involved, and those who are fit to do so must be made to perform war service. The atmosphere of war must be felt by everyone. (...) It is absolutely unacceptable that frivolity [and] neglect should be the prevail in the rearguard...[4]

The POUM was against creating a "regular army," like the Popular Army, if it was going to mean the reconstitution of the old "bourgeois" army. However, the party was in favour of organizing a regular army, which would be the "Regular Revolutionary Army of the Proletariat." The militias would form the basis of this revolutionary army.

This new Army would follow in the footsteps of the historical experience of the great revolutions—in England, France, or Russia—during which armies were formed imbued with the forms of struggle and political ideas of the new dominant social class. The POUM's model was the Red Army of the early years of the Russian Revolution. Consequently, the writings of Trotsky and other Bolsheviks on military matters were circulated among POUM members.

The party summarized the differences between a workers' army and the republican Popular Army as follows:

> Workers' Army: Formed by workers. Controlled by the proletariat, employing all necessary military commanders if there are not enough from the working class. Absolute discipline, based on the collective responsibility of the proletariat. Respect for the technical knowledge of the professional officers, [but] under the political control of the workers. This avoids the formation of a military caste. Each worker knows they are fighting for themselves. They know they are fighting for socialism. This certainty gives them the courage and selflessness that the Soviet Red Army displayed during the Revolution.
>
> Popular Army: No class distinction. Collaboration from everyone is welcome. Exclusive military command. Military discipline, with the exclusion of purely working-class

thought. Its purpose is to defend the bourgeois democratic regime, which every worker knows has failed in Spain... ...the bourgeois democrats... will use the Popular Army to stifle all revolutionary activity on the part of the workers. In other words, purely military control will prevail over everything."[5]

The POUM's opposition to a regular bourgeois army did not mean opposition to compulsory military service. Thus, it advocated the recruitment of all men between the ages of eighteen and thirty. However, as a measure of "revolutionary hygiene," only those from the working class would be sent to the front as combatants. Men of bourgeois origins would be mobilized to build fortifications and perform other tasks.

The Lenin Division

With the creation of the Popular Army of Catalonia (EPC), the militia columns would become divisions, structured into regiments, battalions, and companies (formerly *centurias*) and, in theory, with all the necessary sections in a modern army: artillery, machine guns, sappers, communications, and medical services. On 20 January, the Catalan government announced the creation of four divisions: three from the CNT and one from the PSUC. The POUM militias, lacking sufficient resources and material, were recognized as an *agrupación* (grouping). By early March 1937, the EPC had approximately 43,000 troops, deployed on a front stretching over 400 kilometres, from the Pyrenees to Teruel.

The POUM disagreed with the decision to maintain the military organization in accordance with the ideological characteristics of the columns converted into divisions. However, without the support of the CNT for a reorganization along class, and not ideological, lines, the POUM militia had no choice but to maintain its own columns, collectively renaming them the "Lenin Division," despite the party's forces not being officially recognized as a "division".

Among the more than 6,000 combatants in the Lenin Division, there were about 500 international volunteers who played an important role as front-line combatants, as officers, and in the medical services. From at least 28 different nationalities, the largest contingents were German and Italian. There were also sizeable groups of French, British, Belgian, and Dutch volunteers. Sixty percent were anti-fascist refugees, some of whom had already been living in Barcelona before the Civil War. Many of these volunteers were members of left-wing Socialist parties or dissident communist groups.

The first unit of international volunteers, the International Lenin Group, was organized in August at the initiative of representatives of the Trotskyist movement sent to the Catalan capital. It would form the nucleus of what would become the POUM's International Column, which eventually numbered some 200 members and it would play a key role in the clashes around the Barbastro road in September 1936.

In November 1936, when the international volunteers were reorganized, many of them ended up in the new "Josep Rovira Shock Battalion." In addition, specific sections of French, Italian, and British volunteers were organized.

The Shock Battalion underwent rigorous training and was also provided with the best weapons. It was composed of approximately 450 militia, most of them foreigners, especially Germans. It would be used to carry out raids or repel dangerous enemy attacks. Its members had to be members of the POUM, or some other IBRSU-affiliated party. Commanded by a professional soldier, the German Hans Reiter, the Shock Battalion gained a certain reputation for its "fighting spirit, self-sacrifice, and tenacity."[6] It would play a key role in the two major skirmishes involving POUM militias before June 1937: the assault on the Loma de Arascués and the taking of the Loma del Manicomio.

The Arascués ridge, north of Huesca, had been captured by the fascists in December. On 6 January it was retaken by troops from the POUM Shock Battalion. Later, with CNT militiamen, they took the village of Lierta.

The Loma del Manicomio (literally "Lunatic Asylum Ridge"), northeast of Huesca, was one of the key points in the enemy's defensive system. Its conquest was planned as part of a series of actions designed to distract troops from the central front where the Battle of Guadalajara was being fought. In the end, only the POUM troops took the assigned objective, occupying half of the hill for six hours before being forced to retreat, resulting in dozens of casualties on both sides.

Beyond these isolated actions, and others by the CNT and PSUC militias, it was impossible to launch a serious assault against the well-defended enemy lines around Huesca without sufficient air support, artillery, or tanks. Due to this lack of suitable weaponry, the Republican forces would also not have been able to withstand a serious enemy offensive.

In the case of the Lenin Division, this lack of weapons was even more serious and prevented the party from sending more troops to the front. Even when weapons did arrive on the Aragon front, they were generally assigned to PSUC or CNT troops. In January 1937, the Lenin Division had rifles, often quite unserviceable, for 65% of its infantry, compared to 80% in the case of the CNT and PSUC divisions.

Even worse was the lack of automatic weapons. In early 1937, it was reported that the entire Lenin Division had only 25 machine guns. However, except for the Durruti Division, the other EPC units also had few automatic weapons.

There was also a scarcity of artillery on the Aragon front and what there was was of poor quality. In the newly organized EPC, each division was supposed to have six artillery batteries, each with four cannons. At the beginning of the Civil War, the POUM militia had three batteries, but the second battery was transferred to the ERC's Macià-Companys Column. Given that the artillery reported directly to the headquarters in Barbastro, it is questionable to what extent the POUM artillery unit could be considered a party-controlled unit.

The Lenin Division was the only division on the Aragon front with a cavalry unit. Its origins lay in the Alcántara Regiment of the Lepanto barracks in Barcelona. When the barracks became the 'Lenin Barracks', this unit had been integrated into the POUM militia as the Semion Budionni Cavalry.[7] The cavalry unit also lacked weapons and equipment.

Huesca had not been taken solely due to a lack of weapons but also to the absence of "a comprehensive plan … that would force the enemy to defend itself on multiple fronts."[8] In the meantime, in Huesca, following the failed offensive of October 1936, the enemy had further strengthened its defences and military organization.

The problem, at least from the POUM's point of view, was also that the Catalan government was "subordinated to the central government" and "the money the latter was willing to dedicate to support the Catalan war effort was not enough, either to acquire weapons or to establish its own war industry."[9] This "political subordination" was based on accepting the military priorities of the Republican government, with the war effort concentrated almost exclusively in the central zone, rather than launching a serious offensive on other fronts.

"Sabotage" on the Aragon front also originated, according to the party, within the EPC General Staff itself. During the first months of 1937, Republican planes "did not appear for weeks on end, even though our positions were bombed daily," an absence seen as a consequence of the commanders' distrust of the POUM and CNT troops.[10]

1   A Brandlerite Militant, "Three months on the Huesca Front", in *The Spanish Civil War. The view from the Left. Revolutionary History*, Vol. 4, n°1/2 London, 1991, pp. 290-91.

2   *La Batalla* 8.8.36.

3   *La Batalla* 22.9.36.

4   *La Batalla* 11.2.37.

5   *La Batalla* 5.2.37.

6   Coll, Josep and Pané, Josep, *Josep Rovira; Una vida al servei de Catalunya i del socialisme*, Ariel, Barcelona, 1978, p. 119.

7   Famous commander of the Soviet Red Army cavalry,

8   *La Batalla* 7.3.37.

9   Ibid.

10 A Brandlerite Militant, "Three months on the Huesca Front", in *The Spanish Civil War. The view from the Left. Revolutionary History*, Vol. 4, n°1/2 London, 1991, pp. 297-98.

9

Women in the Face of Revolution

The "true pariah in bourgeois society"

In his book *Hacia la Segunda Revolución*, Maurín described the revolutionary party as "the great liberator" of women, "the true pariah in bourgeois society." However, despite some references by the dissident communists of the need to end women's oppression, the importance they gave to the issue was relatively secondary. This situation would only change in 1936 with the mass entry of women into political activity, the workplaces, and, in some cases, the armed struggle.

Like other Marxists, the POUM posed "the emancipation of women" as an integral part of the proletarian revolution. According to *La mujer ante la revolución* (Women in the Face of Revolution), published by the party in 1937, the key to transforming women's lives was their integration into the workplace—with the same conditions and wages as men. Economic independence was "the first step towards complete equality." As a result of this integration into the workplace, women would enter the trade unions and could thus "become informed about their social position, realize that they are not (isolated), that they belong to a powerful class which represents their interests" and as part of this class they were part of the struggle against exploitation and injustice.

For the POUM, a socialist, collectivized society would provide women—and men—with all the support they needed to raise their families, such as crèches and canteens in the factories. It was not a question of choosing between being a mother or a worker "because in the new society there will be no conflict between motherhood and work, since the boss who did not tolerate pregnant women in the workplace would have ceased to exist".

Thus, the construction of socialism would only be possible with "the active collaboration of women." Its establishment depended "in equal proportion on working women and men", as capitalism represented "the exploitation and oppression of our class, of the working class". But although it meant the "*double* exploitation and oppression for working women" there were no exclusively "men's concerns but only common concerns."

"Equal rights", however, would not be automatically conceded by socialism. It could only open up the possibility of them being won through the direct participation of women workers in building it. This participation was even more urgent in rural areas since the situation of women peasants was "a thousand times worse". "Patriarchal customs in the countryside opened the doors wide open to exploitation", thus "the collaboration of women in the community, in the cooperative... freed from the chains which blunted her creative energy", would mean she would "be able for the first time to develop her personal life within the framework of the community" and would become "indispensable".[1]

For the POUM, the model for women's liberation was the Russian Revolution, which had demonstrated that only socialism could create the material conditions for this to happen. Hence, the dissident communists pointed to what they considered the great achievements that had benefitted women in the Soviet Union. Achievements such as the "effective abolition of prostitution" or the fact that, supposedly, many Russian couples lived freely and equally were presented as examples of how, under a socialist system, the situation of women would change dramatically for the better.

But beyond the grandiloquent declarations, the day-to-day reality for women in the workers' organizations remained difficult. In the POUM, men's attitudes towards their female comrades were often discriminatory. The editor of *Emancipación*, the POUM's women's paper, María Teresa García Banús, complained that sections of the party had little interest in carrying out the necessary work among women: "because of a false understanding of the problem, our male members have not collaborated with all the enthusiasm they should have; indeed, in some sectors they have even gone so far as to fight against the recruiting of women". Or, as García Banús wrote elsewhere, "the reactionary prejudice of women's inferiority, of their inability to participate in public life, is so deeply rooted that many of the revolutionary workers themselves do not treat their female comrades in any other way than that which is customary in bourgeois families".[2]

The Organization of Women

Before the Civil War, women's participation in the BOC was limited almost exclusively to grassroots membership, as was also the case in other workers' organizations. Only between 1933 and 1934 was there a woman on the Central Committee: María Recasens. Between 1931 and 1933, there were only two women in the party's electoral lists, compared to forty male candidates.

In July 1932, to strengthen its intervention among women the BOC created a Women's Section (SF), not as an independent organization, but as an integral part of the party. Aside from general propaganda work and attempts to win women to the BOC, many of the SF's activities were those traditionally assigned to women in workers' organizations, such as fundraising for political prisoners or cultural and educational work.

The SF failed in its efforts to recruit more women into the party. This was because, according to many party members, the existence of the Women's Section responded to a "petit bourgeois" concept or, at best, was a kind of "lesser evil." Furthermore, according to the BOC leadership, most of the party's female members did not participate in the SF, whose activities often fell to young, non-party, women, lacking political experience and, in many cases, with a "petit bourgeois mentality." During the Third Congress of the BOC (in June 1933) it was argued that these defects had been present since the founding of the SF and had not been eradicated. The real problem was the shortage of experienced party members working within the SF, which meant that the necessary political agitation among workers and peasants had not been carried out. Given this situation, the Congress decided to dissolve the Women's Section, and replace it with a Women's Propaganda Commission composed of party members of both sexes. The purpose of this commission, while lacking the minimal separate structure of its predecessor, was more or less the same: to develop propaganda and cultural activities to attract women to the BOC.

The JCI, which had opposed the creation of the SF, was quite successful in recruiting young women who believed that the true revolutionary struggle was waged shoulder to shoulder with their male comrades. Antonia Adroher, a leading member of the POUM in Girona, would recall many years later that "we did not consider ourselves feminists... our dream was to fight alongside the men to change society... There was no difference between them and us".[3] In the language of the time, "feminism" was considered a non-revolutionary ideology that separated women from men and, at best, defended women's rights within capitalism without seeing the need to overthrow the system itself. In the first issue of *Emancipación*, Pilar Santiago, the party's main female public speaker during the Civil War would affirm that "the women's movement of the POUM is not going to be like that of the bourgeoisie, a battle of the sexes."

The lack of prominence of the POUM's women members, would begin to change during the war. As the historian Mary Nash points out "the massive mobilization of the population meant a break from the traditional confinement of women to the home and gave them, for the first time, a collective public visibility." During the war, many women "participated in a variety of war activities (such as) building barricades, caring for the sick, organizing relief work, sewing uniforms or knitting, performing auxiliary services, organizing educational and vocational training courses, and working in transport or munitions factories."[4] Others entered political activity for the first time: they joined workers' and Republican organizations *en masse*, while others went to the front with the militias.

In the context of the revolution, and their sudden mass participation in political life, the Catalan government enacted a series of decrees that benefitted women, many of them introduced by Nin from the Ministry of Justice: for example, civil marriage, an equalitarian and simplified divorce procedure, and the propagation of birth control and contraceptive methods. Above all, Catalonia would become the vanguard in Europe in terms of abortion legislation, which it legalized. For the women of the POUM, this decree had "abolished at a stroke a (form) of slavery much older than capitalist society."[5]

In response to the massive increase of women's involvement in political activity after July 1936, the POUM organized a "Women's Secretariat" (SECF) in September 1936. Like the BOC's former Women's Section, it was not an autonomous organization, but rather a branch of the POUM. The members of its local committees and its central committee were appointed by the party. The aim of the SECF was:

> to recruit to the POUM as many women as possible. To promote the formation of a mass revolutionary women's movement which fights together with its class brothers for the total emancipation of the proletariat. To make women understand that without their firm collaboration the triumph of the revolution is not possible.[6]

At the same time, working women were encouraged:

> to help in the transformation of the capitalist economy's outmoded norms into a new socialist structure. It is the duty of the working woman to throw herself into this task with enthusiasm and with the full weight of her personality, knowing that the new society grants her not only economic and social equality with men, but the definitive equality of rights for both sexes.[7]

The SECF distinguished itself from other women's organizations in the Republican zone. Its reading and knowledge of the work of Bolshevik leader Alexandra Kollontai led it to adopt a "much more open and direct" attitude than other women's organizations on issues such as sexuality, birth control, and abortion.[8] According to the SECF, the availability of contraceptives and the freedom to have abortions, in addition to an adequate public health system, would contribute to undermining the double oppression suffered by women. Likewise, the elimination, with the arrival of the revolution, of the Church's influence on education and moral issues was considered by the SECF as central to creating the conditions for a true emancipation of women.

The SECF held its first congress in March 1937, with eighty local sections represented, the most important of which were those of Barcelona, Girona, and Sabadell. However, the Secretariat did not bring together all the women in the party. Around 500 women normally participated in the SECF's activities at the beginning of 1937, the party had almost 40,000 members.

According to the SECF, the most immediate task for women in the revolution was to support the war effort, given that "without women's help, it would be impossible to sustain such a long war, with its many victims and deprivations".[9] In practice, women's "support" for the war, both in the POUM and in the rest of the workers' organizations, meant performing what was seen as "women's" work by society at large. Thus, women party members and sympathizers participated above all in the activities of the POUM's Red Aid, which organized medical services for the militias, assisted refugees and the families of dead or wounded militia, and set up centres for war orphans.

Militiawomen

The presence of militiawomen at the front, especially in Aragon, was one of the most enduring images of the revolutionary effervescence during the first weeks of the Civil War. Hundreds of women broke with the passive and subordinate role assigned to them in a patriarchal society by going to the front. This was 'a radical change' as it 'projected the image of an active, resolute and enterprising woman dedicated to the war effort'. Thus, during the summer of 1936, the heroic figure of the militiawoman 'became a myth and symbol of resistance against fascism'.[10]

But this image of the heroic militiawoman was used more to encourage men to enlist than to attract women themselves. Significantly, women's organizations did not include the image of the militiawoman on their posters. Available sources suggest that most women rejected the image of the militiawoman in her blue overalls. In reality, the number of women who actually took part in combat was 'a tiny minority' and this was only for a very brief period.[11]

Of the 3,883 POUM militia whose pay slips from September to December 1936 have been found, 121 were women. There were probably more, since this data is not complete. It's difficult to know how many of them actually fought, but the few mentions of militiawomen in the POUM press seem to confirm that there were not many of them. This lack of information also does not seem to be due to the party wanting to hide or downplay the presence of women at the front. The few reports that appeared in the party press concerning female combatants among the ranks of the party militia highlighted their courage and example. This was particularly true of the young German woman Margarete Zimbal, who died in combat in October 1936, who the JCI considered a martyr and "the prototype of the revolutionary woman," or of the brave Captain Mika Etchebéhère, the last commander of the beleaguered POUM militia in Madrid.

The description of two young female JCI members from Lleida, Soletat Casanoves and Pepeta Guasc, when they left for the front with the first POUM column, reflects not only the typically heroic language of the time, but also the pride felt by their comrades:

> [They were] tall, thin, and energetic, but with a great flame in their eyes. They wore the bronze helmet, blue trousers, and the blue shirt of the [JCI]. They carried their weapons on their shoulders... Shortly after enlisting, they got into a car and set off. They were two more soldiers in the workers' column... As they passed through the streets, they raised their fists and sang 'The Young Guard' in firm voices... Their example will encourage the worker combatants... an example [for all] to emulate.[12]

Nevertheless, references to the heroism of the militiawomen were often combined with comments alluding to their "femininity." Even the laudatory tribute to Casanoves and Guasc ended with a reference to their "tough exterior, but tender heart."

Even before militarization—which prohibited women's presence in the front lines—both workers' and women's organizations, including the anarchist Mujeres Libres (Free Women), accepted the withdrawal of the militiawomen. At the end of October, the Popular Front government in Madrid approved several decrees aimed at excluding women from military duties. Not all of them complied, but by 1937 the number of women at the front had reduced significantly.

The POUM clearly accepted the withdrawal of women from the front. On 12 September, the newspaper of the JCI in Leida, *Combat* published an editorial asserting that, despite not opposing women's military training:

> the smooth running of the revolution demands that things go back to normal... The women comrades have nothing to do at the front, apart from those who provide medical or other services, and yet they have a lot to do in the rear. It is time we made the change: let the blacksmith go to the forge, and let the women come to make shirts, jumpers, underwear...

Instead of the militiawoman, the "fighting mother" became increasingly the heroine of the rearguard. A mother who fought against fascism to protect her children. She had to convince her sons, but not her daughters, to join the militias to fight. It was not in vain that the POUM daily newspaper in Girona, *L'Espurna*, presented the mother as "the symbolic figure of the militiamen".[13]

Militarization would lead to a "marked sexual division of labour at the front."[14] The women who remained at the front with the POUM, with very few exceptions, dedicated themselves exclusively to "women's tasks" such as cooking or washing the militiamen's clothes. Others still formed part of the medical services, despite having no training whatsoever. María Teresa García Banús would comment that the training of nurses "did not have great results despite the devotion of the doctors, because many of [the nurses] grew tired and stopped attending classes because they considered them to have no practical application."[15] The few foreign women volunteers at the front with the POUM were also involved with the medical services - although in their case their contribution was important because they often had some medical training.

Despite accepting the withdrawal of the militiawomen from the front, the POUM would break with more traditional gender roles by becoming the only anti-fascist organization in Catalonia to provide military training for women in the rearguard. The party's stated intention was to form a women's battalion, although this never materialized, not only due to a lack of recruits, but simply because militarization meant women could no longer participate in military duties at the front. In reality, this training had a more defensive purpose. According to the POUM's English magazine, *The Spanish Revolution*, "All women workers must be familiar with the use of weapons and military terms, not necessarily because we think they should go to the front, but because the time may come when our comrades will be forced to take up arms to defend the cities." [16]

1   Secretariado Femenino del POUM, *La mujer ante la revolución*, Editorial Marxista, Barcelona, 1937, https://eljanoandaluz.blogspot.com/2017/10/ la-mujer-ante-la-revolucion.html

2   *Juventud Comunista* 25.2.37; *Emancipación* 26.5.37.

3   Cited in Coignard, Cindy, *Las militantes del POUM*, Laertes, Barcelona, 2017. p. 139.

4   Nash, Mary, *Rojas. Las mujeres Republicanas en la Guerra Civil*, Taurus, Madrid, 1999, pp. 92, 104-5.

5   Secretariado Femenino del POUM, *La mujer ante la revolución*, Editorial Marxista, Barcelona, 1937, https://eljanoandaluz.blogspot.com/2017/10/ la-mujer-ante-la-revolucion.html.

6   *Emancipación* 20.2.37.

7   Ibid.

8   Nash, Mary, Rojas. *Las mujeres Republicanas en la Guerra Civil*, Taurus, Madrid, 1999, p. 149.

9   Secretariado Femenino del POUM, *La mujer ante la revolución*, Editorial Marxista, Barcelona, 1937, https://eljanoandaluz.blogspot.com/2017/10/ la-mujer-ante-la-revolucion.html.

10   Nash, Mary, *Rojas. Las mujeres Republicanas en la Guerra Civil*, Taurus, Madrid 1999, p. 93.

11   Ibid, p. 96.

12   *Combat* 25.7.36.

13   *L'Espurna* 23.11.36.

14   Nash, Mary, Rojas. *Las mujeres Republicanas en la Guerra Civil*, Taurus, Madrid, 1999, p. 164.

15   García Banús, María Teresa, "Una vida bien vívida", *Viento Sur* no 93, September 2007, p. 11.

16   *The Spanish Revolution* 2.12.36.

10

The May Events

"The Enemies of the People"

Soviet-inspired anti-Trotskyism would become part of the
struggle against opposition to the reconstruction of the
Republican state, the POUM being be the main victim of
this campaign of vilification and slander. In this context, the
Soviet government exerted direct pressure to ensure that the
POUM was not included in the Madrid Defence Junta in
November 1936 and that Nin was expelled from the Catalan
government on 16 December.

The new Catalan government was formed "without
representatives of the workers' parties" – a subterfuge so that
the anarchists could boast that it was a government based on
an alliance between the unions and the petit bourgeoisie.
But the three UGT representatives were also leaders of the
PSUC, including its general secretary, Joan Comorera. The
new government's policies complemented those of the
central government in re-establishing control of the
economy and the military. During the spring of 1937, in an
attempt to disarm the rearguard and control public order,
the Generalitat took a series of measures to dismantle the
control patrols and secure the handing over of all weapons
in civilian hands. However, both the CNT and the POUM

refused to accept these measures. The situation would not be resolved until after the street fighting in May.

For the government of the USSR, it was intolerable that the Spanish revolution jeopardized its attempts to form an alliance with the bourgeois democracies, and that there was also a party present in the Republican zone that defined itself as communist and denounced the counterrevolutionary nature of the Soviet leadership. Consequently, the POUM has been labelled "anti-Soviet," however, like much of the non-anarchist workers' movement of the time, the party actually sympathized with the USSR, but not uncritically. According to the party, the workers' movement had to combine an "enthusiastic defence of the revolution [with] the right to criticize and evaluate," an attitude that, as Lenin had stated, was the best way to contribute to the world revolution. Extending the revolution, rather than holding it back, was, in the POUM's view, the most appropriate way both to defend the USSR and to prevent the victory of fascism.

The campaign against the POUM had already begun before the Civil War. Maurín and the BOC were accused by the PCE of being "Trotskyists". Outside of Catalonia, in the months leading up to the war, the POUM's activities were occasionally subject to violent attacks by PCE members. But it was not until the summer of 1936 that these sporadic accusations, became a fully-fledged political line that followed the directives of an international operation orchestrated by the USSR.

In August 1936, the POUM denounced the execution in Moscow of the old Bolshevik leaders, Kamenev, Zinoviev and others, accused of collaborating with imperialism and fascism, as the "liquidation of the essence of the October [revolution]" that had led Stalin "not only to a radical distortion of the principles of revolutionary socialism, but to the physical extermination of the Bolshevik old guard."[1] Later, the party would request that the Catalan government grant Trotsky political asylum. Two more acts that would convince Moscow of the perfidious nature of the party led by "the traitor Nin, Trotsky's agent in Spain, just as criminal and murderous as he was."[2] The Comintern urged the Spanish and Catalan Communists to intensify their campaign against "Trotskyism." On 11 December, it wrote to them, stating that it was:

> ...necessary to aim for the political liquidation of the Trotskyists, given that they are counterrevolutionary agents of the GESTAPO. After the political campaign, remove them from local government and all other organizations. Suppress their press and expel all foreign elements."[3]

It would not take long to move from "political liquidation" to "annihilation." Thus, in February 1937, the Comintern Executive Committee called for the "complete and final crushing of Trotskyism in Spain." At the meeting of the PCE Central Committee in March 1937, General Secretary José Diaz asked rhetorically:

> Who are the enemies of the people? The enemies of the people are the fascists, the Trotskyites, and the "uncontrollables." ... It is a serious error to consider the Trotskyites as a fraction of the workers' movement. This is an unprincipled group of counterrevolutionaries classified as agents of international fascism. The recent Moscow trial has shown in the light of day that

the chief of this gang, Trotsky, is a direct agent of the Gestapo...[4]

"Fighting against everyone"

The POUM considered its expulsion from the Generalitat as a step towards eliminating all of its political activity in the Republican zone and called for the party's reinstatement in the Catalan government. Nevertheless, Nin, addressing the POUM Central Committee in December, argued that:

> The fact that everyone is against us is the highest praise. All revolutionary parties have grown fighting against everyone.[5]

The fact that the party had grown considerably since the beginning of the war undoubtedly encouraged such optimism. By the end of 1936, the POUM had around 40,000 members, including members of the JCI, compared to 6,000 on the eve of the war. Most of the new members were young Catalan workers and peasants. Outside of Catalonia, the party had a few thousand members in Valencia and hundreds in Madrid. The weak point for the POUM, given the city's great strategic importance, was Barcelona, where, in December 1936, it had only 2,200 members.

Propaganda—both oral and written—played a fundamental role for all workers' and left-wing organizations at the time. The POUM was no exception. In addition to its radio stations in Barcelona and Madrid and numerous meetings held at a local level, the POUM produced a wide variety of newspapers. By early 1937, it published dailies in Barcelona (*La Batalla*), Girona, Lleida,

Madrid, Manresa, Terrassa, and on the Aragon front, as well as a weekly paper edited by the JCI and others in Barcelona (*L'Hora*), Castelló, Figueres, Olot, Reus, Sabadell, Sitges, Tarragona, and Valencia. Other publications came out more sporadically, such as those produced by the SECF, Socorro Rojo (Red Aid), the children's organization Pioneros Rojos (Red Pioneers), local party organizations in various Catalan towns, several military units on the Huesca front and in Esperanto. The party's foreign collaborators published magazines in Dutch, English, French, German, and Italian. The circulation of the party's five Catalan daily newspapers was 85,000 copies per day. In addition, the party's publishing house, the Editorial Marxista, printed a wide variety of pamphlets, both classic Marxist texts and others written by party members.

However, the party's growth could not compensate for its increasing political isolation. The Catalan government's decision in August 1936 to make union membership compulsory, and the CNT's defence of a single "anarchist" trade union federation along with a separate "Marxist" one, drove a mass of previously non-unionized workers towards either the CNT or, especially, the UGT. Given this situation, the FOUS had no choice but to join either the CNT or the UGT, thus dashing its hopes of creating a single, unified federation.

For the FOUS unions, joining the CNT was extremely difficult after the expulsions and inter-union conflicts of the pre-war period. Therefore, they opted to join the UGT, believing they could take over the leadership of what, in Catalonia, was a relatively weak organization. Once this was achieved, the POUM believed it would be possible to raise the issue of union unity with the CNT.

As a consequence of compulsory unionization, the Catalan UGT already had more than 400,000 members by

October 1936, even more supposedly than the CNT. Many of these new members came from the less combative sectors of the Catalan working class, especially white-collar workers and technicians. The UGT even founded an organization for the self-employed and small businessmen, the Small Traders and Industrialists' Guild (Gremi i Entitats de Petits Comerciants i Industrials), which would be at the forefront of protests against the "excesses" of the revolution. The UGT soon became the mass base of the PSUC, and it proved relatively easy for the Stalinists to break the POUM's influence within the unions.

In addition to the isolation and loss of its trade union base, internal division plagued the party during the first year of the Civil War. The BOC already had had a dissident faction that could be characterized as "Catalanist" -- it opposed the construction of a party at state-wide level, and included, among others, Arquer, Coll and Rovira. On the other hand, the former ICE members, schooled in another political culture, were a focus of dissent, especially in Madrid.

Another centre of opposition was in Valencia, where the secretary of the local party, Luis Portela,[6] led a "right-wing" opposition that advocated supporting the Popular Front, opposed criticizing the USSR in the POUM press and demanded the expulsion of the Madrid organization for being "Trotskyist". On the other hand, there was a more "leftist" opposition among the ranks of the JCI and in the Local Committee of Barcelona that criticized the alleged hesitations of the leadership, as well as calling for the expulsion of Portela.

The most radical internal opposition came from Josep Rebull, the administrator of *La Batalla*, who harshly criticized the leadership of the POUM for not having provided the masses with a clear revolutionary alternative, especially in relation to the question of power.[7]

Maurín, as the party's undisputed leader, probably would have managed to smooth over these differences due to his influence among the membership. His absence, besides being a personal tragedy, had disastrous consequences for the organizational and political unity of the new party. Nin, in contrast was distrusted by the former Bloc leaders and had difficulty exercising his political authority. It was hoped that at least some of the divisions afflicting the party would be overcome at the forthcoming congress, scheduled for 19 June 1937. But this would never take place, as three days before, the POUM was suppressed and its leaders arrested.

"The future of the revolution"

In April 1937, *La Batalla* cited Lenin that "there was no middle path between the dictatorship of the bourgeoisie and the dictatorship of the proletariat. All illusions [in that middle path] were nothing more than the reactionary lamentations of the petit bourgeoisie."[8] The POUM's main target of criticism in this regard were the Stalinists, who:

> To justify their monstrous betrayal of revolutionary Marxism… argue that the democratic republic they advocate will be a democratic republic distinct from the others, a 'popular' republic, from which the material basis of fascism will have disappeared. In other words, they scandalously disregard the Marxist theory of the State as an instrument of class domination to fall into the utopia of the democratic State 'above

classes,' at the service of the people, with the aim of [confusing] the masses and preparing for the pure and simple consolidation of the bourgeois regime. A republic from which the material basis of fascism has disappeared can only be a Socialist republic, since the material basis of fascism is capitalism.[9]

Even so, the POUM, despite its Marxist orthodoxy, avoided drawing a direct parallel, as Trotsky and his followers did, between the revolution underway in Spain and the situation in Russia in 1917. As Nin would explain, no "dual power" had emerged in the Spanish state during the Spanish revolution, as Trotsky claimed, because the local committees were not elected by the masses and were very often, in fact, popular front committees representing the entire Left, including the parties of the petit bourgeoisie. Nin was right in his assertion, if the model of dual power was that of the Soviets in revolutionary Russia in 1917. What existed was, in practice, a *de facto* dual power in which there existed, often disconnected from each other, committees that represented the birth of an alternative power to the Republican state. As Grandizo Munis, the leader of the Trotskyists in Spain during the war, would later explain, there was an "atomization of power," each committee was like a "small government."[10]

Nin noted that, unlike the situation in Russia before the revolution, trade unions in Spain enjoyed "great prestige and authority" among the masses and had never limited themselves to only immediate demands but had also played a political role. The Soviets, in turn, had emerged from the need of Russian workers to find some form of representative body, given the absence of solid working-class organizations. In the Spanish state, workers had not created new revolutionary organizations because they still trusted the unions. Recognizing this reality, in early 1937, the POUM stopped talking about the need to create new committees and called for the formation of a "Revolutionary Workers' Front" based on the party and the anarchist organizations, whose task would be to convene a congress of delegates from the unions and "existing committees" in the workplaces and countryside, and at the front.

As a step towards that end, in April 1937, faced with a new crisis in the Catalan government, the POUM proposed the formation of a government made up exclusively of representatives of workers' organizations, which would immediately implement a series of measures of a "socialist character" and prepare for the convening of the congress of delegates from which a workers' and peasants' government would emerge. These measures were embodied in a government programme adopted by the Central Committee at the end of March. They included the socialization of large-scale industry and transport, the nationalization of banking, the municipalization of housing, a monopoly on foreign trade, the formation of an army controlled by the working class, and an immediate offensive on the Aragon front.

But the POUM lacked the strength to lead the seizure of power alone. Before the war, it had hoped that the Socialist left would provide the basis for a mass revolutionary party, but the experience of the first months of the revolution had shattered that illusion. In April 1937, Nin commented that nothing remained of the "revolutionary" wing of the PSOE, that the different Socialist currents were already united in their defence of the Popular Front and were "playing into the hands of the democratic bourgeoisie." The argument for a "single party" was no longer valid after July 1936 as there was no possibility of Marxist unity. Everything depended on the CNT. As Andrade commented:

> The future of the revolution depends absolutely on the attitude adopted by the CNT and the FAI. The possibility of the POUM becoming the great mass party that achieves hegemony in the revolution is limited by the existence of anarchism....[11]

With the outbreak of the Civil War, the Catalan CNT had regained much of the support it had enjoyed in 1931. According to its own figures, the anarchist unions grew from around 140,000 members in Catalonia in July 1936 to 360,977 three months later, roughly a third of the working population. The main problem for the POUM was how to win over, or at least influence, the CNT masses. As Nin insisted, it was a mistake to consider the CNT a homogeneous organization. It was obvious that there were differences between certain sectors, for example, between the Iberian Federation of Libertarian Youth (FIJL) and the CNT leadership. However, as would become evident during the events of May, most of the CNT rank and file remained loyal to the leadership. The dilemma for the POUM was how to build a revolutionary alternative without clashing with the CNT leadership and, consequently, becoming even more isolated.

In the early months of the war, the POUM was quite optimistic about the possibility of establishing closer collaboration with the CNT. At the end of 1936, Nin informed the Central Committee of the existence of a "secret pact" between the POUM leadership and the CNT leaders in Catalonia, dating back to the creation of the CEC and the agreement on collectivization. At the end of April,

Nin again defended what the CNT and the POUM had in common:

> The CNT is a potentially revolutionary organization, despite its prejudices and misconceptions. We are a thousand times closer to members of the FAI, who are not Marxists but are revolutionaries, than to those of the PSUC, who call themselves Marxists but are not revolutionaries. The problem lies in transforming the revolutionary instinct of the CNT into revolutionary consciousness, that the heroism of its masses becomes a coherent policy.[12]

Undoubtedly, the most significant collaboration between the POUM and the anarchists would be the Revolutionary Workers' Youth Front (FJTR), founded in February 1937 by the JCI and the Libertarian Youth, the FIJL. Other anti-fascist organizations, especially the Stalinists, viewed its formation with concern. Soviet reports spoke of the danger posed by the POUM's influence on "extremist" elements such as the FIJL.

The Stalinists' fears seemed to be confirmed when, on 14 February, the FJTR managed to mobilize thousands of people at a rally in the centre of Barcelona. In the following weeks, a network of local committees and a militia column were organized to go to the front. The FJTR was also formed in Valencia, where it received support from a dissident sector of the JSU. In Asturias, former FJS members expressed their sympathy for the FJTR. The latter were uncomfortable with the Communist control of the JSU and its leadership's defence a "new type" of organization that would include all sectors of anti-fascist youth. A proposal that was denounced by the JCI as a further step towards the "republicanization" of the workers' movement.

"The Barricades of Freedom"

During the first months of 1937, the POUM repeatedly warned of attempts to undermine the revolution, in particular, of any attempt to disarm workers in the rearguard. But the POUM leaders overestimated the strength of the revolutionary forces. In late April, Nin argued that it was still possible to seize power peacefully, without resorting to an armed insurrection, given that the balance of power was still favourable to the revolution.

Meanwhile, violent incidents multiplied, especially between anarchist groups and the police and the PSUC. The death of UGT leader Roldán Cortada at a CNT roadblock on 25 April served as an excuse to organize a massive demonstration in Barcelona, deemed "counterrevolutionary" by the POUM, calling for drastic measures against the "uncontrolled" groups. A new Catalan government, formed four days later, set a limit of 48 hours for all "private individuals" to hand over arms in their possession.

In the days leading up to the May events, the POUM warned that the PSUC was preparing "a provocation." The Catalan Communists believed that "before taking Zaragoza, they had to take Barcelona," and they were stockpiling weapons in the rearguard for this purpose. It's not difficult to conclude that the police intervention on 3 May against Barcelona's central telephone exchange, controlled by the CNT since July 1936, was a "provocation" carried out with "premeditation and malice."[13]

Once the armed clashes began, the POUM, despite having serious doubts about the movement's viability, immediately sided with the workers. *La Batalla* declared on the 4 May that "the barricades of freedom have re-emerged all over the city. The spirit of 19 July has once again taken hold of Barcelona."

The party believed it was possible to take over Barcelona and subsequently force an agreement with the Republican authorities in defence of the principal conquests of July 1936. To achieve this, the POUM proposed the creation, together with the anarchist organisations, of Defence Committees in every neighbourhood and workplace, in addition to once again calling for the formation of a Revolutionary Workers' Front.

In an attempt to forge the unity needed, the POUM met with representatives of the local CNT and FAI. But the CNT leadership wanted to end the struggle as quickly as possible. Consequently, its leaders ignored the proposals of the POUM and the most radical anarchist sectors, primarily the FIJL and the Friends of Durruti group, to take control of the centre of Barcelona, the only part of the city still in the hands of the security forces (basically the Republican Assault Guard) and the PSUC.

Juan Andrade was part of a delegation that met with the leadership of the FAI. He later commented that the FAI was:

> completely overwhelmed by events, it was no longer a question of shooting a boss, but of adopting political decisions; faced with the specific situation, they did not know what to do, but they did retain the haughtiness and self-sufficiency peculiar to anarchists in all circumstances, and above all when faced with 'Marxist politicians'.... I left the FAI premises convinced once again that anarchist

confusionism always culminates in the greatest of political catastrophes."[14]

The pathetic call to the workers by anarchist minister, Juan García Oliver, to "lay down their arms and embrace their enemies" was enough to give the CNT leadership in Barcelona the excuse to retreat completely. The POUM internally recognized that the CNT had betrayed the struggle, but once more the party feared losing touch with the anarchist rank and file.

> Tactically, we must make this criticism with caution, so as not to isolate ourselves. If the CNT leadership were attacked head-on, the CNT rank and file would rise unanimously in its defence.[15]

Unprepared to publicly break with the CNT leaders, the POUM was forced to abandon the barricades to avoid "bloody repression." Such was the fear of being losing contact with the CNT leadership that when the JCI, along with the FIJL, organized a column in the Gràcia neighbourhood to take over buildings in the city centre still in the hands of the Generalitat, the party leadership blocked the initiative. It also opposed the party's Barcelona Committee when it proposed electing Defence Committees at the barricades.

The POUM leadership even presented the results of the May days as a victory, insisting that the counterrevolutionary provocation had been crushed by the magnificent reaction of the working class. Above all, the events had revealed the true nature of the PSUC as "the vanguard and instrument of the bourgeois counterrevolution."[16]

However, there was no reason for such optimism. As POUM Executive Committee member Enric Adroher (*Gironella*) commented a few months after the end of the war that his party had failed:

> to understand the course of events up to May and had therefore not prepared for the struggle and did not know how to take advantage of the great betrayal of anarchism. Instead of presenting [the situation] as it was: a violent struggle for power [the POUM] presented it as a simple counterrevolutionary provocation.

It was not just a provocation, but "the definitive solution" to the contradiction that had emerged in July 1936 "in favour of the counterrevolution."[17]

Trotsky and the POUM

As we have seen, Trotsky, strictly following the Bolshevik model of 1917, had been highly critical of the POUM for its alleged support of the Popular Front and its participation in the Catalan government. He was convinced that it would have been possible to seize power in May. Once again, the POUM, by failing to lead the proletariat in the struggle to seize power, had demonstrated its "centrist" character, vacillating between revolutionary politics and reformism. By late 1937, Trotsky concluded that the POUM:

> by their general 'left' formulas [had] created the illusion that a revolutionary party existed in Spain and prevented the appearance of the truly proletarian, intransigent tendencies.

> [Consequently] contrary to its own intentions [the POUM] had proved to be... the chief obstacle on the road to the creation of a revolutionary party.[18]

However, at the beginning of the Civil War, Trotsky did not rule out the possibility of winning the POUM over to his positions, despite all his criticisms of the party's politics. Many POUM members, especially those from the ICE, sympathized with Trotsky, especially in his fight against Stalinism and the POUM press continued to publish his articles. But Nin's entry into the Generalitat and his refusal to allow Trotsky's followers in Barcelona to form a faction within the party led to the definitive break between the Trotskyist movement and the POUM.

For Trotsky, the May events confirmed the political bankruptcy of the POUM, given that:

> If the Catalan proletariat had seized power in May 1937, they would have found support throughout all of Spain. The bourgeois-Stalinist reaction would not even have found two regiments with which to crush the Catalan workers.[19]

However, in May 1937, the objective circumstances were not as favourable as Trotsky believed. In reality, by then, the Republican government had numerous loyal military forces to call upon.

With the Civil War more or less over and given the magnitude of the defeat of the working class, Trotsky concluded that:

> if the POUM had not marched at the heels of the anarchists and had not fraternized with the

Popular Front, if it had conducted an intransigent revolutionary policy, then... in May 1937... or most likely much sooner, it would naturally have found itself at the head of the masses' and would have ensured victory.[20]

These statements must be put into context. With the steady rise of fascism, the imminence of world war, and Stalinism's dominance over large sectors of the international workers' movement, it was clear to Trotsky there was an urgent need to build a new revolutionary leadership, not only in each country but also internationally. He was confident that "during the next 10 years the programme of the Fourth International will become the guide of millions and these revolutionary millions will know how to storm earth and heaven."[21]

As veteran British Marxist Duncan Hallas commented, "the mood of expectation induced by such statements made sober and realistic assessments of actual shifts in working-class consciousness, alterations in the balance of class forces, and tactical changes to gain maximum advantage from them (the essence of Lenin's political practice) extremely difficult for Trotsky's followers", as did an emphasis placed on the centrality of programmatic demands as a way of overcoming the revolutionaries' weaknesses, whereby the demands in themselves appeared to have "some value independent of revolutionary organization".[22]

In the Spanish state, what Trotsky considered as the lack of revolutionary leadership led him to place all his hopes in the small group of his followers, the Bolshevik-Leninist Section of Spain. Thus, in the spring of 1937, he declared that "outside the line of the Fourth International there is only the line of Stalin–Caballero".[23] Unfortunately for

Trotsky, the official Spanish Trotskyist group would never have much more than thirty members, almost all of them foreigners.

In May 1937, the only time he directly responded to Trotsky's criticism of his party, Nin commented that:

> Nothing is more anti-Marxist than applying to all events and all revolutionary situations a scheme prepared in advance and valid for all cases and all latitudes. The pseudo-Marxists who resort to this procedure, instead of starting from concrete situations to develop the most appropriate tactics, seek to subject them to the scheme, a kind of universal panacea that, when administered, produces completely negative results... But Marxism, which is not a dogma but a method of action, rejects formulas for acting on living and changing reality. The fundamental thing is revolutionary strategy; as for tactics, they must be adapted to reality. Obviously, this is more difficult than mechanically repeating a formula.[24]

1   *La Batalla* 28.8.36.
2   Cited in Elorza, Antonio & Bizcarrondo, Marta, *Queridos camaradas. La Internacional Comunista y España 1919-1939*, Planeta, Barcelona, 1999, p. 363.
3   Cited in Volodarsky, Boris, *El Caso Orlov. Los servicios secretos soviéticos en la Guerra Civil Española*, Crítica, Barcelona, 2013, pp. 163-64.
4   Diaz, José, *Tres años de lucha* Vol. 2; Editorial Laia, Barcelona, 1978, p. 184.
5   *Boletín Interior órgano de información y discusión del Comité Ejecutivo del POUM*, n°1, Barcelona, 15.1.37.

6 Portela had been, with Andrade, one of the founders of the first Spanish Communist party in 1920, which fused with a second split from the PSOE, the Communist Workers Party, to form the PCE in 1921.

7 See: Rebull, José, *La vía revolucionaria* (edited by Agustín Guillamón), Editorial Descontrol, Barcelona, 2017.

8 *La Batalla*, 20.4.37.

9 "Proyecto de Tesis Política", Boletín Interior órgano de información y discusión del Comité Ejecutivo del POUM, Barcelona, 5.4.37.

10 Munis, G., "Significado histórico del 19 de julio", *Contra la Corriente*, México, August 1943, reproduced in: *Balance* (http://es.geocities.com/ hbalance2000/), Cuaderno n° 5, octubre de 1997.

11 *La Batalla* 15.4.37.

12 *La Batalla* 26.4.37.

13 Pagès, Pelai, *Andreu Nin. Una vida al servicio de la clase obrera*, Laertes, Barcelona, 2011, p. 357.

14 Cited in ibid, pp. 358-9.

15 "Reunión del Subsecretario Internacional del POUM, 14 de mayo de 1937. Informe del camarada Gorkin sobre las jornadas de mayo", reproducido en: *Balance*, Cuaderno n° 2, June 1995.

16 Manifiesto del Comité Central 12.5.37. (written by Nin), Nin, Andreu, *La revolución española*, Editorial Fontamara, Barcelona, 1978, p. 289.

17 *Gironella* (Enric Adroher), "Sobre los errores cometidos por el POUM", POUM, *L'experience Espagnole* París, 1939.

18 Trotsky, Leon, "The Lessons of Spain: The Last Warning", 17 December 1937, and "The Culpability of Left Centrism", 10 March 1939, *The Spanish Revolution*, Pathfinder, New York 1973, pp. 318, 345.

19 Trotsky, "A Test of Ideas and Individuals Through the Spanish Experience", 24 August 1937, *The Spanish Revolution*, p. 279.

20 Trotsky, "The Culpability of Left Centrism", 10 March 1939, *The Spanish Revolution*, p. 346.

21 Trotsky, Leon, "The founding of the Fourth International", 18.10.38, *Writings of Leon Trotsky 1938-39*, Pathfinder, New York, 1974, p. 87

22 Hallas, Duncan, *Trotsky's Marxism*, Pluto Press, London 1979, pp. 103-4.
23 LD Trotsky, "Is Victory Possible in Spain?" 23 April 1937; 'The Insurrection in Barcelona', 12 May 1937, *The Spanish Revolution*, op cit, pp262, 266.
24 *Juillet. Revue internationale du POUM*, n° 1, June 1937, Barcelona/Paris (translation by Agustín Guillamón).

11

Counterrevolution

The Suppression of the POUM

The May events represented a turning point in the decline of the social revolution that had erupted in July of the previous year. It would be the last major act of struggle between the defenders of Republican order and the forces of the revolution. "Republican order" was restored, and the balance of power shifted decisively in favour of the counterrevolution. The establishment on 18 May of a new Republican government headed by the moderate Socialist Juan Negrín, without Largo Caballero and the anarchists, was a central part of this process. Largo's opposition to the Communist proposal to outlaw the POUM contributed decisively to his removal.

The central government assumed control of public order and military policy in Catalonia, effectively ending Catalan autonomy. A wave of repression was unleashed against the most militant sections of the workers' movement. A torrent of slander was heaped on the POUM, which was blamed for the May putsch. Among other unfounded accusations, the Stalinists insisted that the POUM militias had abandoned the front and returned to Barcelona. It was no longer just a question of "collaboration" with fascism; the POUM was also now described as "a fascist organization" as such.

Direct repression of the POUM, given the weakness of the local party, had already begun in Madrid well before the May events. In early February, the Junta of Defence confiscated the EAJ-POUM radio station and suppressed the Madrid POUM's daily newspaper, *El Combatiente Rojo*.

On 6 May, the UGT decreed the expulsion of all POUM members; on the 12th, the party was expelled from the Department of Defence of the Generalitat; on the 28th, *La Batalla* was suspended, and all other POUM press was suspended in the following days. The arrest of foreign collaborators of the party also began, including the young and well-known Scottish militant Bob Smillie, who would die in Valencia in suspicious circumstances. It was only a matter of time before the Republican State, urged on by the Communists, attempted to permanently eliminate the POUM from political life. Meanwhile, the party's political isolation grew even more pronounced when, at the end of May, a plenary session of CNT delegates voted for the FIJL to withdraw from the FJTR.

On 16 June, the Executive Committee met legally for the last time. The Second Congress was finally scheduled for three days later. The previous day, the government had decided to repress the party as an accomplice to fascism, thus preventing the congress, and another scheduled for a month later with international delegations, from taking place.

On the 17 June, the Barcelona police headquarters announced that "special agents" from Madrid, had uncovered "a significant espionage network." They had made "a considerable number of arrests, including a contingent of highly dangerous foreign citizens and figures from a particular political party."[1]

Some 300 POUM members, including most of the leadership, were arrested in the following days. By the end of 1937, according to the party, there were around 1,000 people associated with the party in prisons and *checas* ("unofficial" jails) in the Republican zone, the vast majority in Barcelona. The wave of repression was directed not only against the POUM, but also against the most radical sectors of anarchism. Between May 1937 and the summer of 1938, some 4,000 anti-fascists, most of them from the CNT, were imprisoned in Catalonia.

The repression was largely carried out by the newly organized Special State Information Department (DEDIDE), which was effectively run by foreign Communists, often agents of the Soviet secret service, the NKVD. The operation against the POUM was coordinated by the Russian Alexander Orlov, head of the NKVD in the Spanish state between late February 1937 and July 1938. NKVD agents and collaborators were allegedly primarily responsible for the mistreatment and torture suffered by those detained in the *checas*.

Andreu Nin was among the first arrested. He was kidnapped by a group of police officers, JSU members, sent from Madrid for that purpose, after leaving the Executive Committee meeting. Accompanied by NKVD agents, they took Nin to a prison in Alcalá de Henares. On 22 June, Nin was kidnapped by a supposed German Nazi group disguised as members of the International Brigades. The PCE newspaper, *Mundo Obrero*, reported on 25 June the "escape of the bandit Nin," detailing how he had been taken to the fascist zone.

The truth is that Nin was transferred to a "secret" prison, a chalet elsewhere in Alcalá de Henares. But there, as before, it proved impossible to get Nin to confess to his connections to international fascism. Faced with this situation, and perhaps aware that they would never be able to bring him to trial because the "evidence" of his contacts with fascism would not hold up, or perhaps because doing so would have revealed Nin's deplorable condition after weeks of interrogation, Orlov decided to liquidate him. Everything indicates that it was the Lithuanian NKVD agent, Josifas Grigulievich, who carried out the crime.

The Republican government was unable to explain Nin's disappearance beyond the information provided by Negrín that he had been abducted by Nazi agents. What was the most significant political crime to occur in the Republican zone during the Civil War would be highly embarrassing for a regime eager to present itself to the world as a legitimate liberal democracy with full legal guarantees. The persistent international campaign over the case and in solidarity with the POUM probably helped prevent more party members from ending up like Nin.

Even so, there are a dozen or so known cases of POUM members being murdered, including the Basque José M.ª Arenillas, killed by the Communists during the retreat from Euskadi; Marcià Mena, political commissar of Lleida castle, who was shot, accused of organizing meetings with other Republican soldiers; and Francesc Pina, shot in the Omells de Naia concentration camp. Other party members would also be eliminated within the Popular Army. The most well-known cases are those of Josep Hervàs and Jaume Trepat, former leaders of the Catalan UGT teachers' union, who were murdered in March 1938 while serving on the front lines with the 141st Mixed Brigade. Other unidentified POUM members from the same brigade, as well as from the 135th and 140th Brigades, were also shot.

The most notorious case, after Nin's, was that of Kurt Landau, founder member of the Austrian Communist

Party and later an oppositionist, who was responsible for the POUM's international work during the first year of the war. Landau had hidden in the house of party members, where he was arrested by police officers on 23 September 1937. Nothing more was ever heard of him.

Although they were not POUM members, the Russian Socialist Marc Rein, the Czech Trotskyist Erwin Wolf, and the German Trotskyist Hans Freund also disappeared, most likely victims of the NKVD. Their bodies may well have been incinerated in a crematorium supposedly built in the basement of a building in Barcelona by Stanislav Vauptxasso, "one of the NKVD's leading experts in assassination".[2]

The End of the POUM Militias

As a result of the suppression of the POUM, its militias would be disbanded, but not before passing through a test of blood and fire that has been barely mentioned in the history of the Civil War and the revolution.

After the fighting in March 1937, the Huesca front remained more static than ever, apart from the occasional skirmish, such as the attack by POUM militia against enemy positions near the Ermita de Salas, described by Orwell in *Homage to Catalonia*. Meanwhile, the enemy had significantly reinforced its defences around the city. The militias, lacking adequate weapons, had no choice but to hold out in their own trenches, which were, incidentally, much better equipped and constructed than Orwell portrayed them.

In June, an offensive was finally organized against Huesca, with the aim of drawing enemy troops away from their assault on Bilbao. Meanwhile, the former POUM

Lenin Division had been reorganized as the 29th Division, with the definitive incorporation of the Catalan troops (formerly the EPC) into the Republican Popular Army after the May events.

To launch the offensive, some 10,000 combatants, including troops from the International Brigades, as well as abundant military equipment, were sent from the central front. Since its troops were not trusted for political reasons, the 29th Division was initially assigned secondary tasks in the battle plan.

The offensive began on 12 June with the main attacks on the fascist lines west of the city. But after three days of intermittent fighting, the Republican forces had achieved little and suffered heavy casualties. The troops of the 29th Division, despite the intentions of the General Staff, had entered into action east of the city and in the early hours of 15 June, the Shock Battalion participated in a failed assault by on the Loma Verde, located to the north of Huesca.

On 16 June, the same day the POUM was suppressed in the rearguard, about a thousand troops from the 29th Division were sent to capture the Loma de las Mártires. The ridge was a strategically important position in the fascist defences, heavily fortified and previously considered impregnable, stretching a kilometre from the Ermita (hermitage) de las Mártires, located on the northern edge of the city.

After taking the position, the militia endured three days of constant aerial and artillery bombardment, as well as repeated attacks by enemy troops. This was the closest the Republican troops came to the city during the 18-month siege. Abandoned to their fate, with almost no support from Republican air force and artillery, it was impossible to maintain their position, so they were forced to retreat with 40% casualties, including dead, wounded, and missing.

Meanwhile, the Republican offensive had petered out, achieving almost none of its objectives, with the notable exception of the taking of the Loma de las Mártires. It had failed due to a lack of coordination among the commanders, the lack of surprise in most attacks, and the misuse of equipment available.

Despite their sacrifice and heroic conduct, the POUM militias continued to be slandered, especially in Stalinist sources, as collaborators with fascism. On 21 June, the commander of the 29th Division, Josep Rovira, was summoned to Barcelona, where he was arrested. This was the first step in disbanding his division and arresting other officers and militia members, accused, like Rovira, of being "accomplices of the enemy." Many of the POUM division's soldiers joined other units, with which they fought until the end of the war.

A Moscow Trial in Barcelona?

The persecution of the POUM can only be understood in the context of the Stalinist purges in the USSR and their echoes in Western Europe. The same psychology of repression used to unmask the "enemies of the people" in the USSR would be applied by Communist-controlled counterintelligence agencies in their efforts to uncover "fascist agents" within the POUM's ranks. The persecution of the party was based on three preconceived assumptions: that sabotage and treason explained any failure of the war effort, that agents of fascism were behind the sabotage and treason, and that these agents were often "Trotskyists."

Behind this campaign was the method of "amalgamation", prevalent in the persecution of alleged dissidents in the Soviet Union, where anyone opposed to the Stalinist regime was in the service of imperialism and fascism, if not their direct agent. Relocated to the situation in the Spanish state, it would be "obvious" that any person or organization that opposed the Popular Front, whether fascist or revolutionary, was on the same side. The blatant contradiction between the accusations levelled against the "Trotskyists" and reality largely explains the failure of this approach in the Republican zone, where the legal system remained more or less intact. Faced with this reality, the counterintelligence services opted to fabricate evidence or resort to extrajudicial procedures.

The trial of the POUM leadership, conducted by the Central Tribunal of Espionage and High Treason, took place between 11 and 29 October 1938. The result was a resounding failure of the Stalinist campaign to have the leaders convicted as enemy agents. The flimsy "evidence" of their complicity with fascism, fabricated by Orlov and his agents, was unsustainable. The court determined that there was no evidence of any contact between the defendants and Spanish or international fascism. Instead, the accused were convicted for their alleged actions as revolutionaries during the events of May 1937 when they had "tried to exploit [the situation] to carry out their aim of seizing power... to establish the social, economic, and political regime they advocate." Consequently, the POUM and the JCI were formally dissolved, and the defendants were sentenced to harsh prison terms.

The Communists were furious at the verdict. In the highest echelons of the Soviet Communist Party, it was commented that "this scandalous sentence, apparently handed down by the POUM, clearly demonstrates the atmosphere in which the court proceedings took place". A trial which described "spies" as "anti-fascists".[3] The contrast between the accusations, the multiple arrests, and the surprising outcome of the trial could not have been clearer.

There were two main reasons why there was no Moscow trial in Barcelona: the defendants' refusal to confess and the perseverance of the Republican legal system. However, this did not mean that justice was above political interests. The POUM trial was severely tainted by the constant slander it was exposed to and the repression of an anti-fascist organization with thousands of members still fighting on the front lines in the midst of the Civil War. Furthermore, few people learned of the outcome of the trial, as the Republican censor prevented the publication of the verdict. Just over two months later, Barcelona would fall into the hands of Franco's army.

Survival

After June 1937, with its leaders arrested, its premises occupied by the security services, and its press suspended, the POUM reorganized itself. A new Executive Committee was organized, and soon a clandestine weekly edition of *La Batalla* and a new JCI publication, *Juventud Obrera*, were being published. Party leaflets regularly appeared on the streets and in factories. Women and younger activists played an active role in this propaganda effort. In January 1938, the Italian Communist leader Palmiro Togliatti, sent to the Spanish state as a representative of the Comintern, reported that the POUM "remains strong, and is carrying out very dangerous underground work in the factories."[4]

In prison, POUM members organized protests with other anti-fascist prisoners over their situation and the lack of legal proceedings related to their cases. In the Barcelona Women's Prison in November 1937, party members led a hunger strike to insist that their cases be clarified. Socorro Rojo supported the prisoners and their families.

Until the spring of 1938, the authorities were unable to halt the POUM's activities. However, as the military situation worsened, pressure mounted on the party. In March, the police destroyed the clandestine offices of Socorro Rojo, confiscating the food and clothing stored there. In April, the members of the new Executive Committee were arrested, and the party's underground press was permanently suppressed.

With the collapse of the front and the proximity of Franco's troops to Barcelona, prison surveillance was weakened, allowing many anti-fascist prisoners to escape. Among them was a group of POUM leaders who left the Modelo Prison on the night of 24 January for the border in a truck thanks to the intervention of the prison director, a Socialist. At least some of the other POUM prisoners also managed to escape. Others were not so lucky and were among those executed by the fascists in the following months.

The odyssey of exile, imprisonment in French and German concentration camps, and fighting in the anti-fascist resistance would then begin. In 1941, the POUM leadership in France was subjected to a new trial, this time by the collaborationist Vichy regime, and ended up being sentenced to long prison terms for being members of a "communist organization."

In the post-war period, the party struggled to survive. In 1945, an important split led by Josep Rovira formed the social-democratic Moviment Socialista de Catalunya. The POUM remained active in clandestinity in Catalonia until the early 1950s. Afterwards, it existed as a party in exile until the 1970s. With the end of the Franco regime, a valiant attempt to re-establish the POUM in the Spanish state failed. The last issue of *La Batalla* was published in May 1980.

1   Cited in Durgan, Andy, *Voluntarios por la revolución. La milicia internacional del POUM en la Guerra Civil Española*, Laertes, Barcelona 2022, p. 333.

2   Andrew, Christopher & Mitrokhin, Vasili, *The Sword and the Shield: The Mitrokhin Archive and the Secret History of the KGB*, Basic Books, New York, 1999, p. 74.

3   Pagès, Pelai, "El POUM durante la Guerra civil: la obsesión del estalinismo", introduction to Rieger, Max, *Espionaje en España*, Ediciones Espuela de Plata, Sevilla, 2007, pp. 14-5.

4   Togliatti, Palmiro, *Escritos sobre la guerra de España*, Crítica, Barcelona, 1980, p. 182.

12

"The Only Party of the Revolution"

Of the many independent communist groups that emerged internationally in the 1930s, the POUM was the most important. As a party, it was quite distinct from other workers' organizations in the Spanish state. Ideologically, its theoretical grounding contrasted to the intellectual poverty of Spanish Marxism at the time. Unlike its official Communist rivals, the POUM was a relatively open and democratic organization. It modelled its internal regime on what it considered to be the true essence of Leninist democratic centralism, which had been betrayed by Stalinist counterrevolution.

The POUM's goal was to become, first in Catalonia and then in the rest of the Spanish state, the political vanguard of the working masses. Although the Civil War cut short this ambition, there is no doubt that achieving this objective would have required the party to overcome a string of serious obstacles. Among them were its inability to break the hegemony of anarchism over the most militant sectors of the Catalan working class, the short time the party had to consolidate itself after its foundation, just ten months before the revolution, and its weak base at a state-wide level.

While, hypothetically at least, the party, as Trotsky argued, could have chosen another path in the face of the challenges it confronted, such conjecture cannot be divorced from considering the specific characteristics of the Spanish revolution.[1]

The first problem, even before the revolution, was the tendency, first of the BOC and then of the POUM, to overestimate their own strength and, consequently, to underestimate that of its rivals. As early as 1931, when the CNT was at its most powerful, the BOC had announced that it was going to win over the Confederation to communism and, shortly afterward, that the FAI was "finished" as a force in Catalonia.

The POUM was conscious of its need to expand outside of Catalonia if it wanted to become the leadership of the working class. Hence, in the years immediately before the Civil War, the dissident communists tried to win over sections of the Socialist left rather than the anarchists whose sectarianism had proved a barrier to any form of constructive relationship. With hindsight it is clear that this orientation was mistaken given, in the first months of the Civil War, the resurgence of the CNT and the almost complete abandonment by the Socialist left of its "revolutionary" politics.

From the very beginning of the revolution, it was clear that without the CNT, it would not be possible to create an alternative power to the bourgeois state and, therefore, ensure the victory of the ongoing revolution. Since calls to form revolutionary committees in the workplace, in the countryside, and at the front proved futile, the POUM, aware that the Bolsheviks had not built the soviets but had instead pushed them to take power after they had already been organized by workers, peasants, and soldiers, sought an alternative that took into account the situation in the Spanish state. Thus the POUM opted to call for the formation of a government of workers' organizations that would convene a congress of delegates from existing committees. Although it is clear that such a position had a propaganda value, its chances of success depended on the CNT.

Aware that the rank and file would not easily break with the CNT leadership, the POUM, at least publicly, ended up being overly cautious in its criticism of it. Rather than the "socialist programme" of the Catalan government and its "working-class majority," fear of losing contact with the CNT leadership was the main reason why the party ended up participating in the Catalan government. With few exceptions, after being ousted from the government, the POUM leadership refused to see that the party's participation had not only done nothing to strengthen the revolution but had actually helped the counterrevolutionary forces destroy it. The party was tied to the CNT leadership's decision, after July 1936, to collaborate with the Popular Front. A course of action by the anarchist leaders that would play an absolutely central role in rebuilding Republican authority and, consequently, in the fatal weakening of the revolution.

Julián Gorkin, a loyal party leader unconnected to the more critical sectors of the POUM, would summarize in August 1939 the dilemma the party had faced in relation to the CNT. Given that the POUM had not been able:

> to address, either theoretically or practically, the problem of Power and, consequently, of the organs of Power [...] obviously forced it to follow in the wake of other forces, primarily the CNT, instead of heightening the difference within its ranks and thereby drawing at least the

most advanced and revolutionary part of the great confederal organization behind us.[2]

Another problem was that the POUM had been founded shortly before the revolution. Although the POUM grew in the months following its setting up in September 1935, there was not enough time to consolidate the new party before the outbreak of the Civil War. On the eve of the war and the revolution, the POUM was politically quite alone. Relations with other Catalan Marxist parties had been severed. It had failed to influence the Socialist left. Worse still, a significant segment of this left—the youth—had drifted towards Stalinism. The Workers' Alliances were not revived, despite the POUM's efforts. Finally, in Catalonia, the CNT had fought against the newly founded FOUS as a competitor, forming alliances with the UGT against it, and thus broke several of the trade union united fronts that had until then been led by the POUM. In the early days of the war and the revolution, unity prevailed on the streets and at the front, but it would not last.

Trotsky, in August 1940, in one of his last writings, commenting once again on the failures of the POUM, insisted that, based on the experience of the Bolsheviks:

> ... during a revolution, that is, when events move swiftly, a weak party can quickly grow into a mighty one provided it lucidly understands the course of the revolution and possesses staunch cadres that do not become intoxicated with phrases and are not terrified by persecution.[3]

But it was necessary for a party of these qualities to "*exist long before the revolution*, given that the process of cadre formation requires considerable time, and the revolution leaves no time for it."[4] Time, which the POUM did not have.

The lack of a base outside Catalonia was another crucial problem that hampered the POUM's aspirations. The outbreak of the Civil War thwarted its hopes of expanding at a state-wide level, as the party's various groups outside Catalonia had had little time to consolidate their influence. This represented a severe blow to the POUM's strategy. Maurín attached great importance to this expansion after October 1934, when he saw the absence of a mass revolutionary party as the main reason for the insurrection's failure. Hence the insistence on Marxist unity that led to the founding of the POUM.

For the POUM to build a mass proletarian party in Catalonia it also needed a base in the main industrial centres, especially Barcelona. The towns and workplaces where the party enjoyed the greatest presence were, in most cases, far from the Catalan capital, and generally lacked the social and political relevance necessary to have a decisive influence on the class struggle.

Despite its minority status compared to anarchism and, increasingly, to the PSUC, the POUM played a significant role during the first year of the Civil War and the revolution. Its participation on a day-to-day basis in the revolutionary process, both in the rear and at the front, and its political support among a considerable segment of the working class, would make it impossible to re-establish the authority of the Republican State in Catalonia without eliminating the POUM from political life.

The POUM was, as Nin claimed at the end of his report to the expanded Central Committee in December 1936, the "only party of the revolution."[5] Nin, at least, understood what he was confronted with, the scope of events, the great historical moment. The possibility of changing the course of events was another matter, but he was aware of the harsh reality and what was at stake. As he declared before thousands of people at the Olympia Theatre in Barcelona on 10 April 1937:

> The reformists, the Republicans, also say they want to make a revolution. But they tell you they want an orderly, well-made revolution; Lenin also came up against people who wanted a revolution in Russia made by educated, clean workers. These people think the revolution is like a train which arrives on time at the station, and then the stationmaster says: 'gentlemen, we have arrived at the social revolution...' Revolution is not, cannot be like that. Revolution is a harsh, violent thing, full of horrors and uncontrolled groups. One must inevitably go through all this to create a new order.[6]

The victorious outcome of the revolution was in the hands of the working masses. As Nin had exclaimed at another major rally seven months earlier:

> "Woe to us if we do not know how to take advantage of this opportunity! History does not offer such opportunities very often."[7]

1   For example, for a discussion of Trotsky's critique of the POUM,
    see: Durgan, Andy, "Marxism, War and Revolution: Trotsky and
    the POUM", *Revolutionary History*, n°9, Vol. 2 London, pp.27-65.
    https://fundanin.net/2019/02/15/marxism-war-and-revolution-
    trotsky-and-the-poum-andy-durgan-2006/

2   Gorkin, Julián, "El error fundamental", POUM, *L'experience
    Espagnole*, Paris, 1939.

3   Trotsky, "The Class, the Party and the Leadership" (unfinished), 20
    August 1940, *The Spanish Revolution*, pp. 362-363.

4   Ibid. pp. 358-59.

5   *Boletín Interior órgano de información y discusión del Comité Ejecutivo
    del POUM*, n°1, Barcelona, 15.1.37.

6   *La Batalla* 11.4.37.

7   Nin, Andreu, *El proletariado español ante la revolución en marcha*,
    Editorial Marxista, Barcelona, septiembre, 1936.

Chronology

1910

Foundation of the CNT.

1917

Russian Revolution.

1919

March

Foundation of the Communist International.

1921

July

Foundation of the Red International of Workers' Unions.

November

Foundation of the Communist Party of Spain.

1923–1930

Dictatorship of Primo de Rivera.

1924

October

Foundation of the Catalan-Balear Communist Federation/FCCB.

1930

February

Foundation of the Communist Opposition of Spain/OCE.

1931

1 March

Foundation of the BOC.

14 April

> Declaration of the Second Republic.

1932

March

> The OCE becomes the Communist Left of
> Spain/ICE.

April

> Foundation of the Iberian Communist
> Federation/FCI.

10 August

> Failed military coup.

9 September

> Agrarian reform and Statute of Catalan Autonomy
> approved.

1933

11 January

> Anarchist revolt.
>
> Casas Viejas massacre.

30 January

> Hitler becomes Chancellor of Germany.

19 November

> Victory of the Right in elections.

December

> Anarchist revolt
>
> Foundation of the Workers Alliance of Catalonia.

1934

28 March

> Foundation of the Asturian Workers Alliance.

5 June

> Peasant strike.

4 October

>CEDA enters Government.

>General revolutionary strike declared.

>Creation of the Asturian Commune.

6 October

>Catalan Republic declared.

18 October

>Asturian Commune surrenders.

1935

29 September

>Foundation of the POUM.

1936

16 February

>Electoral victory of the Popular Front.

March

>Land occupations commence in the south.

April-July

>Fusion of the Communist and Socialist Youth/JSU.

2 May

>Foundation of the Workers Federation of Trade
>>Union Unity/ FOUS.

17-18 July

>Military uprising.

19-20 July

>Rebels defeated in Barcelona and Madrid.

21 July

>Creation of the Central Committee of Antifascist
>>Militias/CCMA.

>First Moscow trials against old Bolshevik leaders.

4 September
> Largo Caballero becomes President.

September
> Formation of the Women's Secretariat of the
> POUM.
> Stalin decides to send miliary assistance to the
> Republic.
> Comintern decides to organize the International
> Brigades.

9 September
> First meeting of the Non-Intervention Committee.

26 September
> CNT and POUM join the Catalan government.

October
> First volunteers of the International Brigades
> arrive.
> Militarization of the militias. Popular Army
> formed.
> Female militia withdrawn from the front.

24 October
> Catalan Decree on Collectivization.

4 November
> CNT enters the government.

8 November
> Battle for Madrid begins.

16 December
> POUM expelled from the Catalan government.

1937
February
> Foundation of the Revolutionary Workers' Youth
> Front.

3-8 May
>   May events.

18 May
>   Juan Negrín named President of the Republican
>   government.

16 June
>   POUM suppressed.

June/July
>   Andreu Nin murdered.

17 July
>   Dissolution of the 29th (Lenin) Division.

August
>   Suppression of the Council of Aragon.

1938

February
>   CNT returns to the Republican government.

April
>   Arrest of the second POUM Executive Committee.

11-29 October
>   Trial of POUM leadership.

16 November
>   End of the battle for Ebro.

1939

26 January
>   Barcelona falls into the hands of the fascist army
>   Catalonia falls. Hundreds of thousands of people
>   flee to the French border.

1 April
>   End of the Civil War.

Abbreviations

IBRSU: International Bureau of Revolutionary Socialist Unity or London Bureau.

BOC: Bloque Obrero y Campesino/Workers' and Peasants' Bloc.

CCMA: Comité Central de Milicias Antifascistas/Central Committee of Antifascist Militias.

CEC: Consell d'Economia de Catalunya/Economic Council of Catalonia.

CEP: Comité Ejecutivo Popular/Popular Executive Committee (Valencia).

CNT: Confederación Nacional del Trabajo/National Confederation of Labour.

EPC: Exèrcit Popular de Catalunya/Popular Army of Catalonia.

ERC: Esquerra Republicana de Catalunya/Republican Left of Catalonia.

FAI: Federación Anarquista Ibérica/Iberian Anarchist Federation.

FCC-B: Federació Comunista Catalano-Balear/Catalan-Balear Communist Federation.

FIJL: Federación Ibérica de Juventudes Libertarias/Iberian Federation of Libertarian Youth.

FJS: Federación de las Juventudes Socialistas/Federation of Socialist Youth.

FJTR: Frente de la Juventud Trabajadora Revolucionaria/Revolutionary Workers' Youth Front.

FOUS: Federación Obrera de Unidad Sindical/Workers' Federation of Trade Union Unity.

GABOCS: Grupos de Acción del BOC/BOC Action Groups.

ICE: Izquierda Comunista de España/Communist Left of Spain.

JCI: Juventud Comunista Ibérica /Iberian Communist Youth.

JSU: Juventud Socialista Unificada/United Socialist Youth.

NKVD: Narodnyj komissariat vnutrennich del SSSR/ Soviet secret pólice.

PCE: Partido Comunista de España/Communist Party of Spain.

CPSU: Communist Party of the Soviet Union.

POUM: Partido Obrero de Unificación Marxista/Workers' Party of Marxist Unification.

PSOE: Partido Socialista Obrero Español/ Spanish Workers' Socialist Party.

PSUC: Partit Socialista Unificat de Catalunya/ Unified Socialist Party of Catalonia.

SECF: Secretariado Feminino/Women's Secretariat (POUM).

SF: Sección Femenina/Women's Section (BOC).

UGT: Unión General de los Trabajadores/General Union of Workers.

Bibliography

Alba, Víctor, *El marxismo en España*, 2 tomos, B. Costa-Amic Editor, México 1973.

Alba, Víctor (ed.), *La revolución española en la práctica. Documentos del POUM*, Ediciones Jucar, Madrid 1977.

Andrade, Juan, *Notas sobre la guerra civil*, Ediciones Libertarias, Madrid 1986.

Coignard, Cindy, *Las militantes del POUM,* Laertes, Barcelona, 2017.

Durgan, Andy, "Marxism, War and Revolution: Trotsky and the POUM", *Revolutionary History*, n°9, vol2 London, pp.27-65.
https://fundanin.net/2019/02/15/marxism-war-and-revolution-trotsky-and-the-poum-andy-durgan-2006/

Durgan, Andy, *Comunismo, revolución y movimiento obrero en Catalunya. Los origines del POUM*, Laertes, Barcelona, 2016.

Durgan, Andy, *Volunteers for the Revolution. The International Militia of the POUM in the Spanish Civil War*, Brill, Leiden/Boston, 2026.

Gutiérrez, Pepe, *Retratos poumistas*, Espuela de Plata, Sevilla, 2006.

Maurín, Joaquín, *Hacia la segunda revolución*, El Perro Malo, Toledo, 2023.

Nin, Andreu, *La Revolución Española*, El Viejo Topo, Barcelona, 2008.

Orwell, George, *Orwell in Spain*, Penguin Books, London, 2001.

Pagès, Pelai, *El movimiento trotskista en España (1930-1935),* Ediciones Península, Barcelona, 1977.

Pagès, Pelai, *Andreu Nin. Una vida al servicio de la clase obrera*, Laertes, Barcelona, 2011.

Pagès, Pelai; Pastor, Jaime; Romero, Miguel (eds.), *Juan Andrade (1897-1981),* Viento Sur, Madrid, 2011.

Solano, Wilebaldo, El *POUM en la historia. Andreu Nin y la revolución española,* Los Libros de la Catarata, Madrid, 1998.

Tosstorff, Reiner, *El POUM en la Revolución española,* Laertes, Barcelona, 2025.

Trotsky, León, *The Spanish Revolution (1931-39),* Pathfinder Press, New York, 1973.

About the publishers

RESISTANCE BOOKS is a radical publisher of internationalist, ecosocialist, and feminist books. Resistance Books publishes books in collaboration with the International Institute for Research and Education (https://iire.org/), and the Fourth International (https://fourth.international). For further information, including a full list of titles available and how to order them, go to the Resistance Books website.

info@resistancebooks.org – www.resistancebooks.org

 Click on the QR code for Resistance Books

THE INTERNATIONAL INSTITUTE FOR RESEARCH AND EDUCATION is a centre for the development of critical thought and the exchange of experiences and ideas between people engaged in their struggles. Since 1982, when the Institute opened in Amsterdam, it has organized courses for progressive forces around the world which deal with all subjects related to the emancipation of the oppressed and exploited. The IIRE provides activists and academics opportunities for research and education in three locations: Amsterdam, Islamabad and Manila. The IIRE publishes Notebooks for Study and Research in several languages. They focus on contemporary political debates, as well as themes of historical and theoretical importance.

iire@iire.org – www.iire.org

www.ingramcontent.com/pod-product-compliance
Lightning Source LLC
Chambersburg PA
CBHW031559060326
40783CB00026B/4150